SUE BARTON: VISITING NURSE

Henry Street wasn't quite real to them yet. Sue had been advised by the superintendent of her school of nursing to take up Public Health work after graduation – for the very good reason that Sue liked people, and had a definite talent for teaching.

'Public Health work,' Miss Matthews said, 'is one of the most important branches of nursing. I believe that you are unusually fitted for it, and I would suggest that you go to the Henry Street Visiting Nurse Service, in New York.'

Helen Dore Boylston

SUE BARTON: VISITING NURSE

RED FOX

A Red Fox Book
Published by Random Century Children's Books
20 Vauxhall Bridge Road, London SW1V 2SA
A division of the Random Century Group Limited

London Melbourne Sydney Auckland
Johannesburg and agencies throughout the world

First published in Great Britain by
The Bodley Head Limited 1941

Red Fox edition 1991

Set in Times New Roman by Speedset Ltd,
Ellesmere Port

Printed and bound in Great Britain by
Cox & Wyman Ltd, Reading

ISBN 0 09 975190 9

Contents

1
The Little House

Not many of the houses looked prosperous and most of them were grimy; yet the street had charm, for traces of another era lingered in the crookedness of windows and doors, in the casual little yards, in old-fashioned wooden porches elaborate with scrollwork. New York roared around the street and above it. An icy wind from the harbour swept through it, blowing paper into the faces of pedestrians, and tearing at the 'To Let' sign swinging over the door of the smallest house on the street – a tiny red brick house with green shutters and a white door.

The sign creaked dismally, and the caretaker, coming out of the basement of the adjoining house, looked up with an expression of melancholy indifference. Then he glanced along the street and brightened. He could always tell when people were house-hunting, because they progressed so jerkily, pausing every few steps to appraise house fronts and read signs.

The two girls coming towards him were proceeding after this method, and their faces had the set look of people whose feet are beginning to hurt. They were pretty girls, and smartly dressed, but they were not New Yorkers if the caretaker was any judge. New Yorkers always gazed upward, admiring New York, while strangers never did so – for fear of seeming unsophisticated. The Empire State Building was near by, its slender shaft glittering in the sun, yet neither of the girls gave it a look, a long, pleased, neck-stretching look, as any New Yorker would have done.

The caretaker looked them over as possible tenants.

Country people who dressed like that were well-to-do, and thought Greenwich Village romantic. Besides, these girls had young, open faces. They'd believe anything – at least, the red-headed one probably would. Red-headed girls were always jumping at things. Good-looker she was, too, with that white skin and them teeth. The other didn't seem such an easy mark. She had a swing to her shoulders and a kind of snippy nose, turned up and freckled. Her eyebrows looked as if she'd laugh at you if your hat blew off. Anyway, they both had class, and maybe –

When the girls reached the house they paused.

'Oh, look, Kit!' exclaimed the red-haired girl. 'It's like something out of an old book!'

The other girl's reply was quite in keeping with the caretaker's estimate of her.

'Certainly!' she said. 'A nice expensive old book! Listen, Bat, you simply can't have a whole house in New York. You might as well face it. George told you this morning that rents in the Village were out of the question – and they are.'

'But, Kit –'

'Oh, come on! I'm practically dead. Let's go back to the East Side, if we can –'

'Yes – we can go down in the lovely, lovely underground, so warm and fragrant! And, of course, it's perfectly ducky having strange men put their knee in your back and push. I –'

The caretaker cleared his throat. 'Like to look at the house, ladies?'

The girls glanced at each other. 'Well – er –'

The house was as delightful inside as it looked outside. There was one room downstairs, with a fireplace, and french windows at the back opening on a little garden. Upstairs were two tiny bedrooms, a bathroom, and a square landing. The rooms had been newly decorated and were adequately, though not lavishly, furnished. The house was warm and comfortable, and the water in the kitchenette pipes was boiling hot.

'Just the same,' said the red-haired girl sensibly – to the caretaker's surprise – 'what it comes down to is a three-room flat. How is it heated?'

'From the furnace next door, Miss. This house has got a cellar, but there ain't nothin' in it but hot-air pipes.' He added under his breath. 'Anyway, we hope there ain't.'

'What?'

'Nothin', Miss.'

The caretaker was rapidly taking back all that he had thought about red-headed girls. This one was quick – but she wasn't so hasty.

'How much is it?' she asked him, in her pleasant voice.

The caretaker made some hurried calculations. The boss had said let it if possible, no matter at what price, but a good price, naturally – 'It's seventy-five dollars a month,' the man said at last.

The girls stared at him.

'That's without a lease,' he said quickly. '*With* lease it's sixty a month – payable in advance.'

'But why?' the red-head girl asked, her clear honest eyes meeting his steadily.

The caretaker shuffled his feet.

'Why don't we take it, Sue?' the other girl put in. 'We've been hunting for a week, now, and my feet are just ribbons – and there are only two more days before we go to work. We've got to –'

'Wait a minute, Kit.' The red-haired girl turned to the caretaker. 'Will you tell us, please,' she said quietly, 'why the house is only sixty dollars with a lease, and seventy-five without?' She was very nice about it – friendly and direct.

'Honest, Miss,' the caretaker said unhappily, 'it's just that it's awful hard to get folks to sign leases, in February. Spring's comin' along and folks make for the country in summer. They don't want no leases. The boss does better in the long run with a lease, so he's got to fix it so's people will be willing to take it.'

'I see. I'm sorry. I thought –' she hesitated a moment. Then she said, 'All right. We'll take it.'

The caretaker breathed again.

His office was in the house next door. The red-haired girl, signing the lease, wrote 'Sue Barton.' Her friend, 'Katherine Van Dyke.' After 'Occupation' each wrote 'Nurse.'

'Would you ladies give me some references, please – just as a matter of form?'

The girls thought for a moment. 'We don't know many people here,' Sue Barton said. 'But we're going to work at the Henry Street Nursing Service, and –'

The caretaker dropped his pen.

'*Henry Street*! You mean you're goin' to be one of the Blue Nurses?'

'Yes.'

'Oh, lady, lady,' the caretaker moaned. 'Why'n't you tell me? The Blue Nurses took care of my wife when she was sick. I – we – d'you want me to tear up th' lease?'

'Why, no. Why should you?'

The man's eyes were miserable. 'Because I can't play no mean tricks on a Henry Street nurse. There *is* somethin' wrong with the house. I guess you'll think I'm crazy – but – funny things do go on at night – steps – an' screams. There won't nobody stay in it more 'n a week. That's why it's so cheap.'

'You mean – are you *actually* trying to tell us the place is haunted?'

'Well, I dunno what else you'd call it. But nobody wants to stay in it – since early this autumn. We've let it four times, and the people scrammed in a week. Th' police have been all over it, and there ain't nothin'.'

Both girls burst into hearty and delighted laughter.

'That really makes it perfect,' Sue Barton said. 'A ghost! I've always wanted to live in a haunted house.'

'You don't want to live in this one,' the man said morosely.

'Oh, but we do! Honestly, you can't expect us to take this seriously! Do you – yourself?'

'I dunno, Miss.'

'Well, then –'

'Okay, lady. It's up to you. But if you want to get out of it any time – I'll – I'll make it all right for you.'

The girls were still laughing when they went away, after a final excited survey of their house.

'Did you ever see such a sweet little kitchen!' Sue

exclaimed as Kit locked the door and put the key in her purse.

'Are you going domestic on me?'

'Why not?' said Sue lightly, thinking of a day in the future, when the ring she wore on a tiny chain around her neck would have another – a plain band – above it, on the third finger of her left hand.

They discussed their ghost happily in the underground, to the intense interest of such passengers as could hear their remarks above the noise of the train.

'What do you think it is?' Sue asked, clinging to a swaying strap over her head. 'I mean, do you suppose there really are noises there at night?'

Kit grinned. 'Oh my, no! I'm sure it's as silent as a tomb. After all – there are only trains screaming over-head, and trains roaring underneath, and pipes whooping in the cellar, and a lot of ancient stairs complaining about their nails every few minutes – ouch! I'm sorry.' The train, rounding a curve, had flung her against the man behind her.

'Well – but the other houses around are old, too. Why pick on ours to be haunted?'

'How should I know? Maybe it's a hangout for gangsters.'

'Darling! You have such lovely ideas! And anyway, the police have been all over it and found nothing.'

'That's so! But whatever it is – if it is anything – there'll be a perfectly simple explanation for it. There always is.'

'Probably,' said Sue, frankly disappointed at the thought. 'Golly, Kit, it's going to be nice, being a Henry Street nurse. I hadn't realized – I wonder if everybody feels the way the caretaker does, about them?' She was silent a moment. Then, 'I wish Connie were here. She'd adore this. Darn it – why does she have to get married so soon – just when we're beginning to do things?'

'Because she's in love, I suppose.'

'Well, but I'm –' Sue broke off. She had told no one except her father and mother of her engagement to Dr William Barry, who had been an interne during Sue's training-school days. There was no reason for keeping the engagement a secret – except that she had wanted, as she explained to Bill, to 'do things' first. Marriage could come a little later, and she felt vaguely that announcing an engagement was almost like announcing one's marriage. It was so publicly final. Sue meant to tell Kit after a while, but not yet. So her sentence went unfinished. She didn't see Kit's quick, amused glance of perfect comprehension, and both girls fell silent until the train reached their station.

They were staying in Central Park West, with Kit's cousins, Eleanor and George Craig. Sue adored the Craigs. Eleanor was a brisk little woman with a genius for saying the unexpected and irrelevant, and George was an enormous man – not stout, but big – with a great hearty laugh and twinkling brown eyes. His eyes didn't twinkle, however, when he heard the girls' story of their house.

'Sounds queer to me,' he said. 'I wish you hadn't signed the lease until I'd talked to the owner. There's nothing in the ghost story, of course. But something is wrong with the place. An entire house doesn't let, in New York, for sixty dollars a month – or for seventy-five, either – unless something is wrong about it. I'll go down there to-morrow and find out what it is.'

'Yes, do, George,' Eleanor said. 'Because very likely the drains are bad, or the garden is damp. You might notice if the caretaker has a cold. Because, you know, there's nothing worse than a continuous cold for giving people ideas of an entirely wrong kind. You might take him one of those infra-red lamps, George, and a mustard plast –'

The laughter of her three listeners drowned the rest of her sentence – laughter in which Eleanor herself joined heartily.

George did go to see the owner of the house next day, and returned very much relieved, saying that the house was all right. The caretaker's story was correct as far as it went. But the ghost idea, as nearly as any one had been able to tell, was merely one of those superstitions which grow up because of accidental noises, until tenants become a prey to their own imaginings and refuse to stay.

'So you needn't worry,' he told the girls. 'Though I'm sorry for the owner. The thing has made it a bad investment for him. But it's lucky for you.'

Doubts about the house having been removed, the girls prepared to settle in at once, so as to be ready for work the day after the next. They had bought their Henry Street uniforms from one of the three recommended shops which stock uniforms or make them to order. Henry Street nurses pay for their own uniforms, and can do so on the instalment plan if they wish, but Sue and Kit paid at once, not wanting to start out with debts, however small. So there was nothing more to be done about Henry Street except report for duty at the stated time.

Henry Street wasn't quite real to them yet. Sue had been advised by the superintendent of her school of nursing to take up Public Health work after graduation – for the very good reason that Sue liked people, and had a definite talent for teaching.

'Public Health work,' Miss Matthews said, 'is one of the most important branches of nursing. I believe that you are unusually fitted for it, and I would suggest that you go to the Henry Street Visiting Nurse Service, in New York.'

Sue had been delighted. Every nurse knows of the work being done by the Henry Street nurses, and of the struggle of its famous founder, Lillian Wald, to better conditions in the slums. But Sue was still very young – in her early twenties – and busy with graduation and becoming engaged. She had, as yet, no realization of the magnitude of the work she was about to undertake. It was enough to feel that the work was exactly right for her, as an individual. Her ideas regarding the organization of the Nursing Service were very sketchy.

Kit was no better informed in regard to details. She wanted to be an executive, felt that a knowledge of Public Health work would be invaluable, and was willing to accept Henry Street on its reputation and the approval of her superintendent of nurses.

They made their application to Henry Street as soon as they had passed their State Board examinations – a nerve-racking ordeal which took place in the State House and lasted for three days, leaving the girls exhausted, and convinced that they had failed miserably. It made no difference that a graduate from their school had 'never been known to fail State Boards.'

'There is always a first time,' Sue had wailed, 'and I'll bet I'm it.'

But she was not, and neither was Kit, nor Constance Halliday. They all three passed State Boards as they had come through training – together, and with flying colours. But after that Connie left them, to go home, for she was to be married in the summer.

It is hard to break old ties. The three girls had come to the hospital nursing school on the same day, and out of a large class of terrified probationers had instantly gravitated to one another.

Kit came all the way from Canada, a harum-scarum youngster then, and one of a large gamily of brothers and sisters. She had had a magnificient capacity for getting into trouble, and her probationary days were one disaster after another. Even when she was a senior bad luck pursued her, and the girls will never forget the day of 'Willie's slush bath,' nor the episode of Miss Martel and the laundry bag.

Connie came from Chicago. She was a rich man's daughter – a tiny, dark-haired girl with exquisite manners, a bubbling romantic enthusiasm, and the memory of an unhappy home life. For Connie's mother didn't like her, and her father, who adored her, was away much of the time. So she had tried to make a new life for herself in the hospital, and found that nurses do not have great faith in the seriousness of society girls. Connie had a long, hard struggle – which culminated in the famous cockroach's speech on Christmas Eve, her first year.

Sue was a New Hampshire girl, and had turned to nursing as a matter of course, for she had been brought up in the medical tradition. Her grandfather had been a doctor. Her father was a doctor, and her fourteen-year-old brother, Ted, was going to be a doctor – or so he said, and no one doubted him.

In those young days Connie and Kit had looked to Sue for leadership. If she led them into difficulties, she also led them out again; though more than once, in their lively careers, she had, as the girls said, 'rather overdone it – especially when she reformed Francesca Manson, and the night she climbed into the supervisor's window in the Nurses' Home.'

Kit and Connie had guessed that Sue was in love with young Dr Barry before Sue realized it herself, and it was Connie, Sue's room-mate then, who had been so steadying about the whole miserable business of Bill and the Other Girl.

And so, now that Connie was no longer with them, – now that she was marrying Phil Saunders, who had met her by falling down the subway steps on her, – the girls missed her deeply. They had been three so long, in their thinking, that to be only two seemed impossible and unreal.

The excitement of coming to New York, however, was overshadowing everything – even Henry Street, though only two days remained before they were to report for duty. Then, too, there was the added excitement of having a house all their own, subject to no rules about lights out, or the hours for bathing – and possessing the joyful distinction of having a ghost!

It was a simple matter to move. The little house being furnished, they had only to move their trunks and bags from the Craigs' flat, and buy a few odds and ends.

George bundled them into a taxi for the final trip.

'If you hear any screams rending the air,' he grinned, 'or any footsteps running up the walls, just give me a ring, will you?'

'Certainly,' Sue agreed – 'as soon as the phone is in.'

'Well – good-bye! Remember, there's always a place for you at, on, or under our table.'

The girls called back their thanks as the taxi slid away from the kerb, taking them to their new house, new adventures, and a new kind of work.

'This would be perfect, wouldn't it,' Kit said, leaning back, 'if only Connie were here?'

2
'We Say Nothing'

The first evening was spent in unpacking. The little house was silent except for the muffled noises of the city, which could in no way be interpreted as screams or footsteps. The girls slept undisturbed that night. They had no nightmares, and no feeling of a strange presence in the house.

In the morning they finished unpacking and hired a charwoman, and, after lunch, went for a long ride on a Fifth Avenue bus. This was the only thing they hadn't done in the way of entertainment. George and Eleanor had taken them to the theatre, to smart shops, to night clubs, to Chinatown and Harlem. They had been to the top of the Empire State Building and had seen all Manhattan spread out before them. They had tramped for hours over the hard floors of the Museum of Natural History.

So it was pleasant, for a change, to sit comfortably in the bus while it rumbled through Fifth Avenue's traffic and turned off presently to follow the sweeping curves of Riverside Drive.

They had dinner that night in a little restaurant round the corner from their house.

'Maybe the ghost will turn up to-night,' Sue remarked cheerfully as they left to return home.

'It's already turned up,' Kit said. 'It took my bed-room slippers. At least, I haven't been able to find them.'

But she did find them when she was undressing – under the wash basin in the bathroom.

'So that settles that,' she said, disappointed. 'I was all set for trouble, too.'

Their sleep was undisturbed as before, though they went about hopefully, looking under beds and into cupboards before they settled for the night, 'just in case there's a clue.'

The following day, after lunch, they got out their new uniforms, to report at the Henry Street headquarters in Park Avenue.

The uniforms were attractive – well-cut blue dresses with detachable white collars and cuffs, black Windsor ties, warm, grey-green coats, and plain black felt hats.

Henry Street was beginning to be a reality.

'Ready, Sue?' Kit called at last, from across the little landing that separated their bedrooms.

'Almost. There must be some way to make these cuffs stay fastened – but it would take a whole research department to find it! I'll bet the ghost has been tampering with them – they –'

'Never mind.' Kit appeared in the doorway, looking very nice but very unlike herself in the uniform coat and hat. 'Hurry up, Sue. We'll be late. Keep your coat on and nobody'll notice your cuffs.'

It seemed strange to go out in the street in uniform and the girls felt stiff and self-conscious in the underground until they discovered that no one was taking the slightest notice of them.

The offices at 99 Park Avenue were the administrative and teaching centre for Henry Street, and the written instructions sent to the girls had stated that an introductory talk would be given at two o'clock on that day. The girls assumed that they were not the only nurses beginning work at Henry Street, and the assumption was fully justified. At least thirty nurses, most of them young and, to judge from their conversation, students at various New York hospitals, assembled in the auditorium. Everyone wore the Henry Street uniform, and the graduates present, including Sue and Kit, were indistinguishable from the others, except for a certain assurance of manner.

Sue and Kit sat down in the back row of chairs, just as the lecturer appeared and the class fell silent. The graduates leaned forward, their eyes bright with anticipation and interest. The students slumped down with resigned expressions.

'Now,' thought Sue, who knew from experience that the tone of a nursing organization depends upon its heads, 'I shall find out what Henry Street is like.'

The speaker introduced herself as Miss Firrell, Director of Education. She was a young woman with a keen, intellectual face and an informal, friendly manner. She spoke, not as one with superior experience speaking to fledgelings, but quite simple as a friend, and she began with the always exciting story of the beginning of Henry Street Settlement.

Many years ago, she told the class, Lillian Wald, then a young graduate nurse, had been sent into the slums of New York to teach a group of mothers how to take proper care of the health of their children. One of the mothers was absent, and in the middle of Miss Wald's lecture a scrawny, crying child had rushed into the room, screaming that something was the matter with her mother, and would the nurse please come.

Miss Wald followed the child to a tumble-down tenement, climbed over piles of rubbish in the passages, and found the mother lying on a heap of rags in a cold and incredibly filthy room. Miss Wald did what she could – which was little – but the shock of seeing the real conditions in the slums roused her to a fury of resentment and determination. She would change those conditions, single-handed if necessary.

She was only a young girl, unknown, one of the many young nurses. She had no money, and scarcely any plan beyond the belief that to change conditions she must have a thorough knowledge of them, and that the only way to acquire this was to live in the slums herself, as neighbour and friend to the miserable and the desperate.

All the world knows the rest of the story: how, with an equally young and inexperienced friend, Miss Wald rented an old house in the heart of the worst district – in Henry Street; how they lived there, nursing sick neighbours, and going out at all hours of the day and night to give any kind of help that might be needed.

In doing this they became interested in the dormant talents and minds of the people around them, and began to keep open house, to teach, to encourage. Slowly and carefully they gathered information about social wrongs, and at last, armed with their knowledge and their splendid young determination, they went to rich friends, and others not so friendly, and demanded aid, in the name of humanity and social justice. They struggled against child labour, vicious

landlords, and crooked politicians. They fought for
good housing, and playgrounds and good schools –
until, one by one, the age-old horrors of the slums
began to disappear.

This was the beginning of the settlement work. The
nursing service was to follow soon after.

Miss Firrell paused.

The listening nurses knew the story, but they heard
it again with quickening hearts, for this was nursing as
they had dreamed it might be, and each wondered if
she would have dared to do what Miss Wald did.

'I suppose,' Sue thought, 'that she didn't seem any
different from anybody else when she was in training.
Probably she got into scrapes – and I'll bet she got
hauled up for being stubborn – and all the time –'

Miss Firrell's voice interrupted these reflections,
speaking, now, of the present aims of Henry Street,
and Sue heard, constantly recurring, the words
'family unit' and 'community needs.'

So far, Sue's nursing had been limited to hospital
work. Families, as such, rarely obtruded into that
world of silent corridors and white rooms. Family
problems were unheard of – except in confidences
whispered to some hurried night nurse, who could do
nothing about them except listen.

But here, it seemed, the family was almost more
important than the patient, and Sue was surprised and
interested to learn that when a Henry Street nurse
went into a home she was required to keep a record of
every member of the family, and to help with all their
problems, physical, emotional, or financial.

Sue's eyes sparkled. This would be wonderful!

The lecture room was silent except for Miss Firrell's

quiet voice, saying words which took instant root in Sue's mind.

'Learn how much you can teach in one visit, how much will be retained, and when to stop. . . . To the persons on the other side of the door you are young and a stranger, but they know your uniform and they respect it. . . . Always think of your work against a background of community needs – do not be afraid to go anywhere in uniform to ask for anything for the good of the city.'

The lecture ended with a brief outline of the organization, which covered three boroughs of New York and was divided into eighteen Centres, which in turn were divided into districts, one to each nurse. There were Henry Street nurses, Miss Firrell said, who had been ten and twenty years in one district, and were now nursing the second generation.

The class filed out at last, free for the day, and full of excited anticipation. In the morning there would be a lecture on general care in the home – but after that the nurses would report to the Centres assigned to them, and go out that very day, into the slums, with an older nurse!

Sue and Kit were to go to Henry Centre, and as they wandered along the corridor to the staircase Sue stopped abruptly.

'Kitten!' she exclaimed. 'Henry Centre – that's Henry Street itself – where Miss Wald began – it's the very house! We'll work there! Gosh, I'm glad!'

'Are you?' said a clear and cordial voice. 'That's very nice.'

The girls turned, startled, and looked through an open doorway into a small office. At the desk, which almost filled the room, sat the slight figure of a woman in a dark blue woollen dress. The dress was not a uniform, but had, nevertheless, an efficient and official appearance. So had its owner, but she had a warmth of understanding in her face and humorous wrinkles around her steady eyes. The girls received the full force of that direct look while they hesitated, glancing at the lettering on the door, which read:

MISS MACDONALD
PERSONNEL DIRECTOR

'You're Miss Barton and Miss Van Dyke,' Miss MacDonald said pleasantly. 'I recognized you from the photographs you sent. We're very glad to have you with us.'

'Thank you,' said Kit; and Sue exclaimed, 'We're so *thrilled* to be here, Miss MacDonald!'

An odd look of withdrawal came into the director's eyes – and then vanished.

'You mustn't,' she said slowly, 'get the idea that the work in Henry Street is all romance and excitement. You must be prepared for a great deal that is dull routine.'

Sue, perceiving her mistake, said quickly, 'But there's dull routine in every kind of work, Miss MacDonald. We're used to it.'

Miss MacDonald's smile ran over into her eyes. 'Then you'll be all right,' she said. 'And I hope you'll like it at Henry Street.'

'I know we will.'

When the girls were half-way down the stairs Kit said, 'That wasn't such a bright remark, Bat, about being thrilled. She's our big boss – and she thought you were one of the sweetness-and-light girls.'

'I was an idiot,' said Sue heartily. 'But all the same, I *am* thrilled, even if it isn't the way she thought. Because, routine or no routine, the – the kind of work it is, alone, is enough to make it exciting. And isn't she a darling! We're going to like this place, Kit.'

Outside in the street they paused to look up at a gigantic poster of a Henry Street nurse in uniform.

'Um,' Kit said. 'She looks as if she'd had a hard day – and where's her hat?'

'She's nobler without it. Nurses are supposed to look like that – all brow, like a tombstone, and kind of a swing-low-sweet-chariot look. What'll we do now?'

'We might go home and change, and wander around and have dinner somewhere.'

'All right, let's! We could go to a movie after. But we ought to get to bed early.'

They followed this somewhat elastic schedule, and came home from the cinema at a little after ten, feeling highly virtuous. It was pleasant to return to their own little brick house. The scrape of Kit's key in the lock had a welcoming sound, and the hall was comfortingly warm when they opened the door. An electric sign somewhere high above Seventh Avenue shone through the front windows, lighting the living-room, hall, and stairs with a cheerful glow.

'There never was a less sinister house than this,' Sue remarked on the way upstairs.

Kit laughed. 'You never can tell,' she said. 'I feel in my bones that something's going to happen.'

'Well – something is – little Susie is going to bed.'

The girls undressed slowly, talking back and forth

across the landing, until Sue heard Kit's bed creak. A moment later her light went out.

Sue read for a while, propped up on her pillows, until the sentences began to run together. She was reminded of her efforts to keep awake on night duty. 'I don't suppose,' she thought, 'that I'll ever get over appreciating how marvellous it is to be in bed at night.' She turned over, yawning, dropped her book on the floor, and switched out the light.

Shortly after, she heard, or thought she heard, a faint brushing sound, but she was too sleepy to be sure. Her eyes closed and she was drifting off into a warm darkness when she heard something which stiffened her in every muscle – a low wailing moan that rose higher and higher to a fearful scream, and then died away to a hideous, whispering sigh.

Sue lay motionless, her jaws clenched, her eyes wide and staring. A second later she heard the patter of Kit's bare feet on the landing. A nightgowned figure appeared in the doorway.

'Sue! Sue! Wake up! You're having nightmares!'

'I – I'm not asleep,' Sue gasped. 'I heard it too – on the landing!'

'G-golly!' Kit quavered.

Sue turned on the light and sprang out of bed. They stood listening, hearing nothing. Then Kit said shakily, 'It – must have b-been a police car going by, outside.'

Sue giggled hysterically. 'W-well – you wouldn't expect it to be going by – on – the landing – would you? And – that sound was in this house!'

'You're telling me! It sounded as if it – came from your room.'

'But it didn't! There's nothing here. Wait – I'll put on the landing light.'

There was nothing on the landing, or in Kit's room. They switched on all the upstairs lights and stood close together at the head of the stairs.

'Shall we –' Sue began, and broke off, staring downward with enormous eyes. Kit's glance followed Sue's. The glow from the electric sign shone up the stairs, and the light from the landing above shone down on them. There was nothing whatever on the stairs.

Sue's hand closed on Kit's arm.

'It – moved,' she gasped. 'Something stepped on it!'

'On *what*?'

'The – the stair – the tread – fifth from the bottom!'

'It *couldn't*, Sue.'

'*Look!*'

They looked down the worn wooden staircase, and while they looked they saw the treads of the sixth and seventh and eighth and ninth stairs spring upward slightly, one after the other, rhythmically, as though released from under a weight. And stair by stair – they creaked!

'It's – coming up here!' Kit breathed, through stiff lips.

But she was wrong. Whatever was on the stair, invisible, came no further. Instead, it stopped on the ninth tread, and the pause was worse than the steps had been.

The girls stood for a moment, wild-eyed. Then they turned and bolted for Sue's room, slamming and locking the door behind them, and flung themselves head first under the bedclothes.

It was some time before they moved. But at last Sue stirred cautiously and pulled the sheet away from her face. The room was as usual. She sat up. Kit was a shapeless lump beside her.

'Come out from under those bedclothes, Van – I know you!' Sue hoped her voice sounded normal. She wiped her damp forehead with the sheet.

Kit sat up and they looked at each other, their faces white in the lamplight, their smiles feeble.

'Where – were you – on the night of February second, Miss Barton?'

'Sitting up with – a friend, your honour.'

They laughed, hysterically at first, then more naturally, reassured by the sound of their own voices.

'We're crazy,' Sue said. 'You can't *have* steps on stairs!'

'I don't want steps on stairs. You take 'em!'

'Not me! Oh, why isn't the telephone in?'

'And just what would you do with it? Give the ghost free telephone service?'

'Don't be silly. Ghosts use telepathy.'

The girls were feeling much better. In the warm, brightly lighted room their panic seemed foolish.

'But what *was* it, Kitten? All this is perfectly impossible! It *couldn't* happen!'

'Well – it did; so what?'

'I don't know. I don't believe it. I mean – I know we heard an awful howl, and thought we saw the stairs being stepped on, but there's some explanation. After all, as you said, it might have been a police car going by with the siren on. With the windows open it could sound inside the house.'

'What about the stairs? Let's see you get round that!'

Sue shook her head. 'I can't. Are you game to go downstairs and look around?'

'Oh, sure,' said Kit, but with a marked absence of heartiness.

They slipped out of bed, unlocked the door, and, wrapped in bathrobes, tiptoed to the head of the stairs.

'What if it's there now?' Sue whispered. 'We'd have to go by it – or – or *through* it!'

'Don't be an idiot!' Kit said, suddenly brisk. 'After all, it was you who suggested going down there, and you've always taken the attitude that it was just a friendly sort of ghost.'

'Yes – but I'd no idea it would be so excessive. What if it has an affectionate impulse and pushes us downstairs?'

'Hooey! Come on!'

Kit went nonchalantly down the stairs – but she kept a firm grip on the banisters. Sue followed close behind. Nothing happened. The girls searched the house thoroughly and found no trace of any intruder, human or otherwise.

'What about the cellar?' Kit asked.

'Darling!' said Sue. 'There's such a thing as overdoing this. The door to the cellar is locked, and if there's anything down there it can stay there. I'm going to bed – and we're going to drag your bed across the landing and put it beside mine. I'm no Joan of Arc. If I'm going to hear anything more in my room that isn't me, I want it to be you!'

Kit was more than agreeable – she was enthusiastic; and they went back upstairs to move Kit's bed, which was smaller and more easily handled than Sue's.

By the time they were settled for the night they seemed quite themselves again; but in spite of their show of bravery they started at every sound, and once, when an unsteady passer-by knocked over a dustbin on the pavement, Kit dived under her pillow, and Sue's jeering laughter had a hollow sound.

'All the same,' Kit said presently from the darkness of her bed, 'whatever this thing is I'm not going to be scared out of this darling little house by it, even if I have to tie a bandage over my jaws to keep my teeth from chattering.'

'Same here! And Kit – we say nothing to anybody about what's happened. Let's pretend that everything's fine. There's no good going to the police. They've been here and found nothing. And I simply can't bear to have that caretaker mooching around being superior and saying "I told you so"!'

'Exactly. And if George and Eleanor found out they'd make us move.'

'What if it happens again?'

'Oof! You would have to bring that up, wouldn't you!'

'Well – suppose it does happen again? Do we still say nothing?'

'It's all right with me,' Kit said steadily.

3
Henry Street

The girls woke to a clear, sunny morning, and a decided feeling that they had been ridiculous. It is difficult to believe in the supernatural when sunlight lies warm on the floor and one is busy making coffee and struggling with perverse cuffs.

After breakfast Kit suggested an inspection of the cellar, and Sue agreed without a qualm.

The cellar steps were under the hall stairs, the door fastened with an ordinary hook. It had not been disturbed. The stairs were concrete, descending to a square cellar which was empty except for the hot-air pipes along the ceiling. These came in from the adjoining house – as described by the caretaker.

'How does he get in here?' Kit wondered. 'There's no door into the next cellar.'

They examined the wall between the two cellars. It was a substantial, wooden partition, solidly built, of wide, old-fashioned planks nailed to beams and uprights. It offered only a blank surface.

'He doesn't get in,' said Sue, 'unless he comes in from upstairs in our house. Besides, why would he want to – except to sweep out once in a while? The furnace is next door.'

'Maybe he's a vampire. Maybe that was his mating call we heard last night.'

'Well, it's wasted on me. I've never cared for men

with howling fits. Anyway, he says he's married.'

'Oh, that wouldn't make any difference to a vampire. They never bother about conventions. What about the windows?'

There were two small windows and a narrow door opening on the garden. The windows were barred on the outside and dusty and cobwebbed inside. The door was heavily bolted.

'Heavens!' Kit said. 'Anybody'd think it was Sing Sing. Not even a mouse could get in here from the outside. Oh, look! There's a cupboard!'

They approached it hopefully, but it was a dis-appointment. It would scarcely have been large enough to have concealed a person had it been empty – and it was full of odds and ends: a mop handle, several empty paint pots, three old and dirty cushions, a stool with one leg broken, and two pails.

'So that's that,' Kit said.

'Yes – and while I don't wish to seem to hurry you, still, we have got a nine-o'clock lecture, and –'

'And it's half-past eight. Come on!'

They went back upstairs, hooking the cellar door behind them, and went on out into the winter cold.

It seemed strange to be going out of doors to go to class, and it would seem stranger still, Sue thought, to be tramping city streets all day long, with no super-visor or head nurse at hand, and tenements wherever you looked.

Sue had never been inside a tenement in her life, and whenever she thought of the afternoon before her she was divided in her emotions: glad that she was going to do this kind of work, and a little frightened at the thought of going into poverty-stricken homes as a

stranger, and perhaps as an intruder. Still, the
caretaker had said, 'I can't play no mean tricks on a
Henry Street nurse.'And if Miss Wald had been
afraid there would be no Henry Street nurses.

The lecture, this morning, was held in a small
classroom, very like the classrooms of a hospital. It
had the familiar bed, with the familiar doll in it. There
was the usual bedside table and chair. But why the
stack of newspapers?

In the few minutes before the lecture began Sue
glanced around the room at the assembled nurses,
and noticed two 'different ones' – a girl of about
twenty-three with straight dark brown hair, alert
brown eyes, and a gay face. Her hat was stuck on the
side of her head, and her manner was casual in the
extreme. The other was fair-haired, neat, and
anxious. She sat on the very edge of her chair. Both
seemed rather odd persons to be Henry Street nurses,
and Sue was wondering how they would turn out,
when the lecture began.

The nurse who gave the lecture was young, and her
manner was different from that of any instructor Sue
had known since she had become a nurse. In the
hospital, the instructors worked with enormous
classes, and had to cover a great deal of ground. They
became, of necessity, crisp and impersonal. This
instructor seemed aware of each nurse in the class,
separately, and she watched their faces individually
for the sudden brightening that meant a desire to
speak, or for the blank look of incomprehension.

The stack of newspapers was explained at once.
They were used for a great variety of things – for
making waste bags, as table covers, as padding for

babies' mattresses, for pillows when a shampoo or an irrigation was to be given and there was no rubber sheet.

The class was told that the first thing to do, on entering a home, was to explain the nursing service to the family.

'Then ask for a newspaper, set your bag on it, on a chair or the table, and remove your hat and coat. The next thing, after you have seen the patient, is to make the paper bag for waste. You need never take newspapers with you. Even the poorest family will be able to get one for you.'

The instructor went on from this to the important subject of the contents of the nurse's bag, and Sue leaned forward eagerly. Almost everyone who has seen the 'blue nurses' on the street has wondered what was in those square, black leather bags which hang from the crook of the arm by double loops, and look so compact and businesslike.

Sue had expected thermometers, cotton, bandages, rubber tubing, and a hypodermic set, and these appeared, but not until an apron and a small bundle of paper napkins had been removed. Then came soap solution and a towel, hand lotion, records, small trays for sterilizing instruments, a white enamel cup, scissors, forceps, and vaseline.

After this general exhibit the instructor put everything back, and began a demonstration of the bag technique.

'There must be no carrying of infection from one house to another,' she said. 'Therefore, the bag must never touch anything in the house. Always set it on a newspaper. Wash your hands before taking out your equipment, and before returning it – sterilized – to the bag.'

The class listened, absorbed, while she removed, in careful order, the articles necessary for a case of general care. She explained the reasons for their being placed on the table always in the same way, produced sterile supplies, and showed them the method of sterilizing a thermometer before and after using. The technique was clear-cut and exact – the result of many years of experiment and elimination. But aside from this the class found that general care in the home was very like general care in the hospital.

Some member of the family was to be instructed to prepare for the nurse's next visit, clearing the kitchen table and covering it with newspapers for the bag, and arranging a tray, makeshift or otherwise, for the bedside treatment and dressings.

The instructor paused a moment, scanning the rows of faces. Then she said: 'Can anyone tell me why it is best to work in the kitchen rather than in the bathroom?'

There was a brief silence. Then the girl who wore her hat so jauntily said, 'Because the kitchen will have water, and a stove for sterilizing things – and because there probably isn't any bathroom.'

'Good. That's exactly it. Nearly always the bathroom is out in the hall of the tenement, and used by many other families. If this is the case, and you have waste fluids to be thrown out, don't let any helpful member of the family throw them into the sink – where dishes are to be washed. There is sure to be a mop pail in the house. Use it, instead. It can be carried out later and emptied.'

These minor details, taken togther, were giving Sue a very clear picture of what her working conditions would be. She had never thought whether there would, or would not, be a bathroom, or realized that she might have to work in a room so bare of furniture that she would have to use a box or a chair for her equipment. This would be the real test of all her years of training. This was the way the nurses in the Great War had to work, making the best of what meagre equipment they had – and that best could be very good, if one had ability.

There was one difference, however – the war nurses had not had to teach. But the Henry Street nurses must combine teaching with their regular work. In fact, teaching was their real aim.

'Do as little as possible, after the first visit,' the instructor told them. 'Let some member of the family give the nursing care while you supervise. Your object is to make the family as independent of outside help as is within reason. If they have some knowledge of home nursing they will not feel frightened and inadequate when someone is sick. They will know what to do while they are waiting for the nurse or the doctor, and, since the nurse's visit is so short, they will know how to keep the patient clean and comfortable between the visits, especially during the night.

'This afternoon you will go out with the older nurses. Watch them carefully to see how they approach the family, how much is being taught, and what has already been learned. In a day or two you will go out alone, on carefully selected cases, and at the end of the week your supervisor will accompany you, to help you with any problems that may come up.

Don't be afraid to ask her questions. She is there to help you.'

This concluded the lecture, and Sue was startled to discover that it was almost lunch time.

Before leaving headquarters the new nurses were told how to reach their Centres, and were given their bags. Sue and Kit went away in growing excitement.

'Why don't we go to Henry Street now?' Kit said. 'There must be somewhere round there to eat – and if we go now we'll have time to get lost.'

'Must we get lost? Couldn't we just go straight there?'

'We can try,' said Kit grimly.

They managed to get off at the right station, and, finding a small cafeteria near by, lunched there before walking the rest of the way.

'It's colder here,' Sue noticed, as they came out in the street again. 'And I can smell the sea.' She was silent for a moment. Then, 'Kit, I'm sort of scared – are you?'

'Yes – a little. I always hate beginnings. You feel so inadequate. And we've never been in homes, before, to do nursing.'

Sue nodded. 'Yes. You feel all exposed and uncertain. I wish it were next week. We'll know more or less what we're about by then. Oh, look! Let's go that way!'

The street Sue had noticed with such sudden interest was Hester Street, and when the girls set out along its shabby length they stepped into a new and noisy world.

It was a narrow street of grey, bedraggled tene-ments, but the buildings were low, and the sun poured down on barrows filled with fruit, vegetables, tools, secondhand clothing, bags of old shoes, cheap sweets, watches, toys. All the odds and ends from the docks, all the city's cast-off and forgotten things, were here. Beams of sunlight filtered through the dusty windows of junk shops on to a clutter of tarnished brass, old clocks, lamps, broken furniture, and synthetic jewellery.

The street swarmed with life in spite of the icy wind. Hawkers bellowed, housewives clamoured, children scrambled shrieking underfoot; old people sat stolidly on tenement steps, their faces impassive but their eyes bright with interest. The smell of fruit, pickled herrings, and the sea mingled with the rich brown smell of roasting chestnuts and blue wood smoke from fires, burning in pails along the gutter. Far up the street, beyond slanting roof tops and rakish chimneys, the slim arc of a bridge span was white in the sun.

Sue's eyes sparkled. Her nervousness was forgotten.

'Why! It's like – like living in an electric current!' she exclaimed. 'And I thought the slums would be dreary!'

They elbowed their way through the crowd, looking and listening, delighted with everything, and Henry Street, when they came upon it at last, seemed yet another world – of quiet integrity.

It was a wide clean street of worn houses, with a few hopeful trees here and there, and a general appearance of tranquillity. In the old days, before Miss Wald came there, it had been a street of dark tenements behind tenements. There had been no drainage, no ventilation, and often no water. The houses had been plague spots – fire traps.

Sue and Kit, knowing this, stared round-eyed at its present state of respectability.

They both saw the House at the same moment, but not until they were almost upon it, for, with the exception of the 'Visiting Nurse' sign over the door, it differed little from the other houses.

Inside, however, it was undoubtedly very different. The girls had a brief impression of a low-ceilinged entrance hall, wood-panelled, and with a green-tiled floor. A telephone operator smiled at them over her switch-board.

'The nurses' office is up the stairs, last door to your right.'

'Thank you.'

The girls hurried upstairs, caught a glimpse of a sitting-room gay with chintz, and found themselves in the doorway of an office filled with long tables, desks, and filing cabinets.

A young supervisor came to meet them.

'I'm Miss Russell,' she said, and Sue wondered whether it was by accident or design that all the Henry Street supervisors were so unusually pretty. Anyway, they all had the same graciousness of manner – it seemed to be a mark of Henry Street.

There were a few nurses working on records at the long tables, and at the far end of the room, standing disconsolate, was the anxious nurse Sue had noticed in class.

Miss Russell introduced the girls and explained the daily routine.

'In the morning,' she said, 'you have about an hour

in which to do whatever clerical work is necessary –
finish records, reply to letters from patients, or
whatever comes up, and collect your list of calls for
the day. You may return here for lunch if you wish –
though the girls usually have lunch in their districts
and telephone the office for any additional calls. You
do not have to return here at five o'clock, but many of
the girls do so, in order to leave their bags, or change
their clothes.'

There were a few other details, mostly concerning
the records – or 'family folders' – which seemed very
complicated to Sue, and filled her with misgivings.
She had no time to express these, however, for almost
before she realized it she was on her way out to the
street again, in the company of an Englishwoman
whose name was Mrs Kirmayer.

Mrs Kirmayer had been twenty-five years at Henry
Street, always in the same district, and she had
worked with Miss Wald, which was sufficient to set
her apart in Sue's eyes.

They set off together down the street. Sue was very
conscious of the weight of the bag on her arm, of her
trim uniform. She was a Henry Street nurse at last!
And Miss MacDonald or no Miss MacDonald, she
was thrilled.

Mrs Kirmayer moved with the steady, swinging gait
of the long-distance walker. She seemed unconscious
of her heavy bag. It was a part of her, as was her
uniform.

The afternoon was a jumble of disconnected
impressions which, taken together, made a clear,
complete picture. There were only general impressions at first: the black line of tenement roofs

against the sky; the sharp cold of the February wind; the smell of sea and smoke; hallways with plaster peeling from the walls; dark flights of shaking stairs; grimy doors; a smell of cabbages and unaired feather beds – and a sudden, sharp picture of Mrs Kirmayer standing on a windy street corner looking up at the tenements. Her hat brim cast a slanting shadow across her steady eyes. 'I love these old streets,' she said.

The words were simple, direct, and undramatic, but they were the summary of twenty-five years of toil and teaching in crowded tenements – twenty-five years of trudging through winter snows and the stifling heat of summers that had vanished, one by one, into a rich past.

Sue felt a little staggered.

'What a – full – life you've had,' she said.

'Yes,' Mrs Kirmayer returned quietly.

Sue watched her at her work and felt ignorant and clumsy. Mrs Kirmayer wasted no moves. Nothing escaped her. Her eyes were everywhere, but she talked to the people as a friend – as one of them. She had a genuine interest in puppies, radios, or new clothes-baskets. She knew how to make the still faces of the old break into wrinkled amusement. She knew about the goodness and the badness of everybody's children. She knew who were in jail and why, and when they would be out. But she did no preaching or moralizing. What was done was done. Her part was to untangle the difficulty now that it existed. It was she who must cure little Johnnie of tantrums, and find a job for the man just out of prison. It made no difference whether the problem concerned a drunken husband or how to fit a second-hand gas range, Mrs

Kirmayer was there with an adequate solution.

One visit stood out especially in Sue's mind. It was not an important case, nor was it unusual. Perhaps this was why Sue remembered it afterwards – it seemed so typical of the way in which Mrs Kirmayer smoothed out other people's troubles.

The case was that of a young couple with a first baby coming, and a neighbourhood clinic had referred the prospective mother to the Henry Street nurses for the beforebirth care.

Sue and Mrs Kirmayer clambered up to the fourth floor of a dingy tenement. The patient was scarcely more than nineteen, a thick-set olive-skinned Italian girl, with curling black hair. Her husband, also Italian, was startlingly blond – sandy hair, blue eyes, and light, clipped moustache. He was doing the family washing when Mrs Kirmayer and Sue came in.

'I couldn't,' he said earnestly, 'let *her* do it, now.'

He had no work, he said, but the landlord was letting them stay on, though they were behind with the rent. No, he wasn't on Relief – he was still trying to get a job. Sometimes he was able to get a day's work as a labourer.

Mrs Kirmayer talked to the girl about her hospital arrangements, made some necessary tests, offered some sound advice, and then asked about clothes for the baby.

There was a flushed, unhappy silence.

'If you'll let me see what you have –' Mrs Kirmayer urged.

Husband and wife looked at each other and looked away. At last the girl said in a pitifully embarrassed voice, 'I – we – we ain't been able to get much.'

It seemed that the baby's layette consisted of four diapers and nothing else. Mrs Kirmayer examined them and approved. Then she sat thinking. After a moment she rummaged capably in her bag and produced a piece of paper, on which she wrote swiftly.

'Take this,' she said to the boy, 'to the Day Nursery at this address. I just happened to go in there this morning, and I noticed that they have one layette left.' She grinned cheerfully. 'I saw it, tucked away at the back of a cupboard, and I thought at the time that it might come in handy. It's a lovely layette – everything you'll need – little dresses, bonnets, woollies, underwear, socks – and they're so pretty. There'll be about two dozen diapers, too. Of course, you have some, but I expect you could use the rest. Just tell them I sent you.'

There was an incredulous silence.

Then the girl cleared her throat. 'L-little dresses?' she said. 'Woollies? A – a bonnet? *Oh!*'

There was a lump in Sue's throat. She glanced at the young husband. All the tenseness was gone from his face, and he was smiling at his wife across the table – with such tenderness that Sue's eyes stung. She spoke hurriedly, trying to talk down the tightness in her chest.

'You're looking forward to the baby, aren't you?'

The two young things, with no money and no future means of support, replied in chorus, 'Oh, *yes*!' The boy added proudly, 'I guess a baby means a lot to anybody – sump'n to work for.'

Sue thought, 'What work, you poor darling!' Aloud, she said, 'Do you want a boy or a girl?'

His eyes grew big. 'It don't make no difference what it is,' he said simply.

Sue was very silent, going down the rickety stairs. Outside, Mrs Kirmayer said briskly, 'I must get him work at once.'

And Sue, after an afternoon spent observing Mrs Kirmayer's methods, had not the slightest doubt that the boy would have a job within the week.

This was the last visit of the afternoon, and 'was thrown in as an extra,' Mrs Kirmayer said, with a sudden twinkle in her eyes.

The other cses had all been selected for Sue's instruction – one new case, one general care, and one treatment – an impersonal list, as empty of the human values involved as Sue's memory was full of them. For the new case had been a girl of Sue's own age, with serious heart trouble, and she lay on a lumpy mattress on the floor of a room without windows. Sue had missed neither Mrs. Kirmayer's skill with the family nor the silent gratitude on the wan young face when Mrs Kirmayer's matter-of-fact voice announced that a 'real hospital bed' would be sent to-morrow.

General care, with bath and bedmaking, was given a very difficult old man with a very difficult beard, and he was moved to delighted blasphemy when Mrs Kirmayer presented him with a beautiful new comb.

The treatment case was a tired little woman with five young children and a burned leg. The dressing of the leg took only a short time, but cleaning up the youngsters and straightening the room, with accompanying cheerful comment, took an hour. Sue helped, glad of an opportunity to do something. She felt subdued and excited, simultaneously. There was, it seemed, a great deal more to the work at Henry Street than she had ever imagined.

'We'll have to save the bathing of a new baby for to-morrow,' Mrs Kirmayer said. 'There isn't time to-day.' This was after the last visit, to the young couple who had needed baby clothes – and encouragement.

On the way back to the office Mrs Kirmayer told Sue about the various relief agencies, private charities, nurseries, insurance companies, and health stations which co-operate with Henry Street. Sue listened with growing satisfaction that she was to be a part of this great network of kindness that spread itself over the city – the largest city in the world.

In the underground, going home with an equally impressed Kit, Sue thought once more of the care-taker's cry that he couldn't play no mean tricks on a Henry Street nurse. And, remembering what she had seen that afternoon, she understood.

4
Puppies and Fish

Nothing whatever happened in the little house that night. The girls waited for the wail, or the sound of something on the stairs, but neither came.

Sue had one more day with Mrs Kirmayer, and made the most of it, trying, in advance, to think what she would do in each case, and then watching to see how Mrs Kirmayer managed. She knew that her first cases would be carefully chosen, that there was little likelihood that she would encounter difficulties, and that if she did she could telephone Miss Russell for advice. But in spite of all this she remained in a state of nervous apprehension.

The full day in Mrs Kirmayer's district was exhausting. Sue was not accustomed to city pavements, or to climbing so many flights of stairs. Long before five o'clock her knees were shaking with weariness. Kit was equally tired.

They limped home from the underground, thankful that they could have dinner in the little restaurant, and that someone else would do the washing up. Kit broke a long silence as they turned down their own street.

'My feet are simply tatters,' she said.

'Do you mean those things hanging off our ankles?' Sue returned. 'If you do, I can only say that you're lucky if you can feel 'em. I can't. I'm just a cluster of fine old well-done knees.'

'Wait till to-morrow,' Kit predicted. 'We're going to be so lame we can hardly move – and when I think of all those stairs!'

The caretaker was on the pavement in front of their little house. He beamed, seeing them in uniform.

'Evenin',' he said, and added anxiously, 'everything all right in the house?'

'Oh, yes!' Sue was very hearty. 'Everything's fine. We're crazy about the house.' This last, she reflected, was true enough – as far as it went. They did love the little house.

'That's good!' the man said warmly. 'I shouldn't want you moidered in your beds.'

'And that,' Kit said as they unlocked the front door, 'will give us something else to look forward to. Do you suppose anything is going to happen to-night?'

'I'll let you know in the morning.'

'Well, if – oh, look! The telephone's in! We ought to ring Eleanor right away. I promised I would, the minute the telephone came.'

Kit dialled the number, and after a moment the receiver crackled violently. 'That's Eleanor,' Kit murmured, quite unnecessarily, for Sue was standing close behind her and could hear every word.

Eleanor's voice crackled and spat. 'How are you, dear? I've been so worried! Not that I believe in ghosts, but they're so unpleasant to have around – and I couldn't bear it if you were murdered in your beds – so distressing –' Her voice went on and on, and Kit grinned, answering.

'That's the second murder to-night,' Sue remarked as Kit hung up.

'Well, why not? There are two of us to be murdered, and there's no use being stuffy about it. Eleanor wants us for dinner to-morrow night.'

'Dead or alive?'

'She didn't say, but I'm sure it will be all right.'

'Not at all! If I can't go up there alive I'd rather stay home.'

'Oh, well, if you insist –'

They went upstairs, laughing, and changed their clothes, their weary legs already beginning to stiffen around the knees. After dinner, with the stiffness increasing by the minute, they attacked the problem of bag technique, practising faithfully as they had been taught, until their heads grew thick and details confused.

'I could do this in my sleep, by now,' Kit said at last.

'You are already doing it in your sleep, if you ask me. And I'm reaching the point where I'm wiping the soap with alcohol and putting the thermometer in the soap dish. Let's stop – huh?'

Kit yawned and grunted. 'I'm ready. I hope the ghost stays away to-night. I'm too crippled to cope with it.'

The little house was silent and peaceful when they went to bed, and, fortunately for the two exhausted girls, it remained quiet and peaceful, so that they fell asleep at once and slept heavily all night, without being disturbed.

The morning was raw and grey, with a smell of snow in the air. Sue was fully lame as she had expected, and so was Kit who seemed depressed. The district around Henry Street seemed very bleak under the heavy sky, and Sue left the office feeling that she had been abandoned by everything that was known and sure.

Her first visit was to a child, home from the hospital after a slight operation. There would be general care to give and a simple dressing to do. That was all.

'Oh, dear!' Sue thought, trying not to limp. 'I wish I'd taken up office work!' She consulted her pocket map. Where was this number – 214?

There are always children playing in the street on New York's East Side, and Sue paid no attention to a patter of feet behind her until a child's voice, choked with tears, called, 'M–miss Nurse! Wait – please – oh, *please*!'

Sue turned quickly, and saw a small boy, dirty-faced and tearful, carrying a puppy, which dangled strangely from his arm.

'What is it, sonny?'

'L–lookit, nurse! M–my dog! *Please* help him!'

'Heavens!' Sue exclaimed. She seized the limp puppy and tried frantically to loosen the strangling cord from about its neck, but it was too strong for her slim fingers.

The child sobbed. 'I – I din' mean to – hurt – him! Th' string got too tight.'

'It's not too late,' said Sue gently, and, holding the puppy under one arm, she tore open her bag, snatched out a pair of scissors, and cut the cruelly tight cord. The puppy gasped feebly, ran a pitifully blue tongue over its black nose, and began to struggle.

'There! He'll be all right now. Haven't you any collar for him?'

'No, I ain't.'

'All right – come on with me.' Sue made for the nearest junk shop, leading the wondering child, carrying the puppy, and followed by a growing procession of youngsters. In the junk shop she bought a collar and lead.

'Here you are,' she told the dazed boy. 'But you'd better carry him for a while, until he feels better – and get him a drink of water right away.'

'Y – yes'm.'

Sue went on, still searching for her number, but the tenements had lost their dreary look. They seemed friendly now – almost gay. 'I guess,' she thought, smiling a little, 'that I wouldn't like office work very much, after all.'

Number 214, located at last, presented her flinching legs with five flights of stairs to be climbed. At the top, panting, she found a warm, cheerful apartment, clean and well furnished. Her bag technique went off more smoothly than she had dared to hope, and her little patient submitted to the dressing without a murmur. When it was done, the child's mother, a stout and lively Irishwoman, offered Sue hot coffee and doughnuts.

'Plaze do have some, nurse. Shure, an' it's a mane cowld day out.'

Sue accepted gratefully, touched by the woman's simple kindness, and sat down, feeling content and suddenly assured. Nursing in homes wasn't too impossibly difficult, after all. And the family had never once suspected that she was as green as grass. She was about to make some casual remark to the woman when the kitchen door was flung open, and a man, obviously the husband and father, said in lusty, cheerful tones, 'Where is she?'

Sue already knew, from the routine questioning of the mother, that the father was a fish dealer, but she was hardly prepared for the ten pounds of fish which he thrust into her lap. Furthermore, Henry Street nurses do not accept presents. What ought she to do? She couldn't hurt their feelings.

A fragment from Miss Firrell's introductory speech slid into her mind with an almost audible click. 'If you cannot refuse a gift without causing offence, accept it for the Henry Street Nursing Service.'

This was splendid in theory, but what, Sue wondered, stifling a grin, would the Nursing Service do with ten pounds of codfish? She had a brief picture of herself doling out chunks of fish in the office – and her grin almost broke through.

The man's broad Irish face was beginning to flush. Sue spoke quickly.

'Thank you so much, Mr Flannigan. Henry Street nurses do not accept presents for themselves, but I would be delighted to take this for the Nursing Service.'

The words, against a background of fish, seemed wholly ridiculous; but Mr Flannigan beamed.

'Indade, an' 'tis glad I am. Ye're a foine lot of gels!'

Sue departed, her bag on one arm and the reeking fish, slithering about in its wrapper, under the other. What she could do with it, and what her other patients would think of a nurse who came in smelling to high heaven of fish, she didn't know. But there it was. She had it, and she'd have to keep it.

Her next patient, approached with some degree of confidence in spite of the fish, was a convalescent influenza – an enormously fat mound of a woman with a deep baritone voice and four Pekingese dogs, which, as Sue told Kit that evening, 'tried to jump up at me after the fish before I'd got inside the door.'

The few bits of furniture in the apartment were good, and Sue guessed that the woman had seen better days. This surmise proved to be correct. The woman's husband had been a prosperous restaurant-keeper. Now he was looking for a job as a barman. 'And we owe so much,' the woman said, 'that we don't have enough to eat.'

Sue paused abruptly, a clean sheet dangling from her hand. 'Do you like fish?' she demanded.

'Why – why – yes, I do. But what –'

'Well – I've got a *lot* of fish, on top of the mantelpiece in your kitchen – where your Pekes can't get it. I'd be only too glad to leave you as much as you can use. In fact, you've no idea how glad I'd be to leave it with you.'

When Sue left her load of fish was several pounds lighter. 'By our presents shall ye know us,' she paraphrased, and burst out laughing in the street. She was no longer nervous, and her first day as a Henry Street nurse was becoming more and more of a success.

Still laughing, she walked on, looking at her next call slip. 'Mrs Levitsky,' she murmured. 'Insulin treatment. I wonder if she cares for fish.'

Mrs Levitsky lived on the top floor back, in a very dark old building. Sue's agonized knees carried her up the stairs, over piles of falling plaster and through variegated smells – coal gas on the first-floor landing, cabbage on the second, sauerkraut on the third, garlic on the fourth. The dingy door on which she knocked, after looking in vain for a bell, was opened by a stout lady with an enormous stomach, snow-white hair, and jet-black bushy eyebrows. She looked so very much like an ageing Airedale that Sue's smile of greeting was somewhat broader than she had intended.

Mrs Levitsky spoke very little English, but her bright old eyes sparkled at Sue, and she talked incessantly. Sue understood about one word in five, but eventually she perceived that Mrs Levitsky was making a complaint about something. Sue felt that the old lady had reason to complain. She was over eighty; she had no family; she was on Relief, and she was a diabetic. Not one of these misfortunes, however, appeared to be the basis of her present trouble. Sue looked round the apartment, which consisted of a quite sunny kitchen and a hole of a bedroom without windows. The kitchen had a table, a chair, and a small stove, on which a single onion boiled optimistically in a large quantity of water.

Sue tried pointing here and there.

Mrs Levitsky shook her head. 'Street!' she insisted, in a very cross voice. 'Street!'

The kitchen windows looked down on a small park, part of a new housing project. A few babies were sunning in their prams, while their mothers dozed, or talked together in scattered groups. It was a pleasant view, with a great deal of sun and space.

'Nice?' said Sue hopefully.

'No nice!' Mrs Levitsky returned with vigour. '*Street!*'

'Oh!' Sue exclaimed, suddenly enlightened. 'You mean you want to see the street?'

'*Ja!* Street!'

The memory of the barrows came back to Sue – Hester Street, and others, with the old people sitting in still contentment on the tenement steps, watching the fights, the love-making, the bargaining. The life they had always known went on around them. They saw it all. They were part of it because they were there. And here was Mrs Levitsky confined to a room from which nothing was to be seen except a park full of prams. Parks were nothing to Mrs Levitsky. She wanted life.

'And,' thought Sue, 'she ought to have it. Maybe I can do something – maybe she could be moved to another room, overlooking the street. I'll ask Miss Russell what to do.' There was no use, however, in raising Mrs Levitsky's hopes, and Sue got out her hypodermic syringe, suddenly businesslike.

When the insulin had been given Sue handed the last of the fish to Mrs Levitsky, whose eyebrows quivered with excitement.

'*Für mich?*' she said, incredulous.

'Yes – for you!'

The knotted, swollen hands trembled, unwrapping the fish. Its clean whiteness was beautiful on the shabby table. Mrs Levitsky looked up at Sue, her eyes quick with tears and bright with pleasure.

'*Danke!*' she faltered. '*Danke!*'

The word rang in Sue's ears as she went down the dark staircase and out into the street – the ugly, lively street that was the universe to Mrs Levitsky, the teeming, sooty street, lovely with life.

'She's *got* to have it!' Sue's sensitive lips were a thin line of determination. 'She's got to! I'll get it for her! Golly, what a morning! If the afternoon is –' She remembered suddenly that there would be no afternoon in the district. She must go to another lecture at Park Avenue.

'And just when I was really beginning to take hold,' she thought, with sincere regret.

5
The First Week

The afternoon lecture was on the care of the new-born, and with the exception of a few suggestions in regard to creating facilities where there were no facilities – such as making a baby's cot out of a drawer – it differed very little from the method Sue had been taught.

When the lecture was over the class was free for the day.

'And do we need it!' Kit said. 'I'm all in! And we have to go to Eleanor's for dinner.'

'Well, I could do with a good dinner. What'll we wear?'

They almost forgot their weariness in the discussion about clothes, and the underground roared them home – still talking, but not entirely about clothes. Their thoughts had returned to Henry Street long before their station was reached, and Kit was deep in an account of *her* morning by the time their little house loomed out of the winter darkness. They were not in an observant frame of mind when they entered the house, or they might have noticed that the cellar door was unhooked. But they didn't see it, and consequently were unaware that the hook was in place again before they went out.

They returned from the Craigs' family early and in very lively spirits. Eleanor had invited two young naval officers for dinner, and the party had been hilarious – with a great deal of laughter, and as much dancing as the girls' fatigue would permit.

The taxi drew up before the little house, and the girls got out, saying good-night on the steps to their too eager escorts.

'It's no use urging,' Kit said. 'We're working goils, and we've got to have our sleep. You can't come in!'

They took a long time getting ready for bed – cold-creaming their faces, examining eyebrows, and chattering. Sue had just turned down her bed and was about to open the window when Kit called to her from the bathroom. '*Sue!*' she said in an odd voice. 'Come here a minute.'

Sue went to the bathroom door. 'Huh?'

Kit was standing before the mirror in her night-gown, her face still smeared with cold cream. She held up her hand. 'Listen!' she whispered.

Sue listened and heard nothing – or was that a faint brushing sound somewhere?

'Hear it?' Kit asked.

'I – I don't know. You mean that little brushing noise – *there it is again!*'

A moment later a screaming wail burst upon them. Sue was standing in the bathroom doorway, which opened onto the landing, and there was nothing on the landing except a single chair. But the sound – the scream – was there, mounting higher and higher, to die away at last in a hideous, whispering sigh.

Sue put out her hand, blindly, and Kit clung to it. Neither of them could speak. There was a brassy taste in Sue's mouth and a coldness along her spine. Kit's face was a greenish-white.

They waited, knowing what would come next, and unable to stir. A full minute passed in dead silence. Then they heard the Step. It began as before, a little way up the stairs, and came on steadily, creaking, to the ninth treat, where it stopped.

Kit's hand tightened painfully on Sue's. That pause of the step was horrible. They felt that It was standing there – looking. But this time they didn't bolt for safety. What was the use? A closed door couldn't stop a thing like that! They stood, rigid and defenceless.

It was a long time before they began to breathe more easily.

'I – I guess that's the whole show – for – the night, isn't it?' Kit said faintly.

'I – guess so.' Sue was shivering in her thin pyjamas.

A sudden shrilling of the telephone, downstairs, tore along their nerves in a pain of shock, but after their first involuntary start neither of the girls moved.

The telephone rang again, and again, commanding, wearing them down. And it was real. It was familiar. It was something tangible and understood.

'Will you – come with me?' Kit said at last.

Sue nodded.

They moved forward, clinging togehter, and paused at the head of the stairs. The telephone still rang, a determined and encouraging sound.

The girls took a deep breath and rushed down the stairs.

Kit's snatch at the receiver cut short a ring.

'H–hello?'

'Boogey! Boogey!' said George Craig's voice. 'How's your ghost?' Sue could hear his chuckle.

Kit gasped, her eyes turning in horror to the empty stairs.

'What's the matter? Did I wake you up?'

'Oh – no. We hadn't – gone to bed.'

'That's good. You've got a letter here, from home. Eleanor forgot to give it to you. Shall I send it down or will you be up and get it? Hello? Are you still there?'

'Yes.' The word was scarcely more than a whisper.

'Hey! Is anything wrong? You sound like a very aged frog.'

'Oh, *George* –' Kit wailed, and then, as Sue's elbow caught her in the ribs, she tried to say brightly, 'Nothing's the matter. You might forward the letter because I don't know just when we'll be round.'

When George had hung up Kit turned on Sue. 'Why didn't you let me tell him? This business is getting a bit too much. I don't like it!'

'S-hh-h! Tell you upstairs.'

Safe in bed, and with the door bolted, Sue explained.

'I was all for telling him myself, for a minute. But look, Kit – suppose there really is – something – or somebody, in the house –'

'Suppose!' Kit sat up violently and stared across her bed at Sue. 'Suppose? And what, may I ask, was all that ghastly uproar on the landing? Maybe you think it was just the house, snoring! Or were we having nightmares in the bathroom?'

'No, but don't you see – whatever is doing this has been doing it for a long time, and to other tenants besides us. And nobody has been hurt or attacked. Nothing has been stolen. If it meant to do anything but scare people it would have done it long ago. And why give ourselves away over the telephone? Let it think we're not a bit disturbed – and then maybe it will give *itself* away.'

'Mm.'

'I don't believe it's any ghost. There aren't ghosts. Somebody wants to frighten us away from here.'

'Yes,' Kit said slowly, 'that's so. And of course George would have a fit. But that scream rattled me so I was –'

'Me too – for a minute – and that's just what it wants, I'm sure. Let's wait just a little longer before we tell anybody. If we could just get used to that thing, so we weren't so scared, and could pay some attention to *how* it happens –'

They had ample opportunity to become accustomed to the scream and the steps before the week was done. The same thing happened four nights in succession, and repetition did dull their fear – as Sue had hoped.

The scream was always on the landing, and was followed by the sound of ascending steps – until the third night, when Sue took her courage in both hands and, when the brushing sound ceased, went half-way down the stairs. She took up her post there, waiting grimly.

The scream came as usual – but the steps did not!

'So we've got a sort of clue,' she whispered to Kit, afterwards.

'What do you mean – clue?'

'Well, when one of us is on the stairs the steps don't come up. That ought to tell us something sooner or later.'

'You listen to it, then. I'm going to sleep under the El structure at night. A nice chummy train, whooping by every three minutes, would be utter peace after this.'

Sue laughed. She was beginning to feel almost indifferent about the ghost, though she was forced to admit that its presence didn't make for restful nights. Both girls were growing hollow-eyed from lack of sleep and increasing fatigue, so that their work suffered – though not too seriously, as yet.

They tumbled out of bed in the mornings feeling stiff and heavy, swallowed a few mouthfuls of scalding coffee, and inched their way over icy pavements to the underground. In its stale warmth, while the train rocketed through the darkness, they came slowly awake, to speak bitterly of the ghost and its activities, or to stare dully at the lights flashing past the train windows.

At the office there was the hour's work on records, and their sleep-starved memories failed them. They made mistakes, rectified them painstakingly, and exchanged looks of united resentment across the long table.

But once outside again, their call slips in their pockets and a razor-edged wind in their faces, their resilient young minds clamped down on the day's work, and they forgot that they were tired.

All the morning Sue tramped the swarming, noisy streets, her bag heavy on her arm. She climbed draughty stairs and knocked at countless dingy doors, discovering in the process that her uniform and a friendly smile were a passport into any dwelling. She made beds, learning how to make one sheet last a week, and that a layer of newspapers between two blankets was as good as a quilt, even if noisier. She found that it was possible to give a bath in an icy room without chilling the patient.

At noon, her back aching, Sue ate lunch wherever she could, often alone, sometimes with another nurse encountered on the street. Then out again, on the afternoon rounds. She washed babies on newspaper-covered pillows. She cleaned canaries' cages and disinfected dogs. She dressed burns and cuts, and learned to save the old bandages, to be cleaned and used again. She discovered that Italian grand-mothers, born in the old country, had obstinate convictions about the care of babies.

When the blue winter dusk fell she straggled home with Kit, satisfied and content. For in spite of the agitated nights Sue was happier than she had ever been before. She loved the shabby old streets. She loved the colour and the noise. And though she was still only a raw beginner, with a great deal to learn, that first week proved to her, beyond any doubt, that Public Health nursing was the only work for her.

Once or twice there was a break in the routine, when the new nurses went to another lecture. Once or twice Sue found that some effort she had made a day or two ago was already producing visible results.

The best of these was the solution of Mrs Levitsky's problem. Sue had talked to Miss Russell about it the day after her visit to the determined old lady.

'Get in touch with the home relief officer for the district,' Miss Russell told her. 'Explain the situation, and ask if the room can be changed on the grounds that the patient's mental health requires it – if you feel that it really does.

The home relief officer was sympathetic, and very

prompt in action. Two days later Sue found Mrs Levitsky in a new room, with an entire market spread before her delighted old eyes. The change in her was very gratifying. She no longer stumped about the room, her face drawn with misery, but sat in supreme contentment before the window. Even her eyebrows seemed less bristly, and her square wrinkled face was quiet and at peace.

At the end of the week Miss Russell went out with Sue for a morning, and Sue found that she had even more to learn than she had supposed.

A day or two before she had treated a woman with varicose veins, and had noticed a curly-headed two-year-old staggering around with an extreme case of bowlegs. Sue advised the child's father to take the boy to a clinic, and on that Saturday morning she stopped, with Miss Russell, to inquire about the results.

The man met Sue and Miss Russell at the door. His face was sullen, and he did not ask them in, but announced briefly that the doctor at the clinic had said that Sammy must have corrective shoes at once.

'And they cost five dollars!' the man said bitterly. 'Five dollars! Them guys must think there's money lyin' around in gutters! I – I brung Sammy home – and I ain't goin' there no more.'

Miss Russell's pleasant voice broke the silence.

'Did you tell the doctor that you had no money?' she asked.

'Naw! What's the good of that? He ain't gonna gimme any, is he? He's gotta have it – to pay his shoffer a hundred bucks a month!'

'If you'd told him,' Miss Russell said, 'he would have sent you to the hospital social worker – and she would have got the shoes for Sammy. Miss Barton, will you give me one of your refer slips?'

Sue hastily produced one. Miss Russell filled it in and handed it to the man. 'Take this,' she said, 'to the social-service department at the clinic.'

'You – you mean they'll *gimme* shoes for Sammy?'

'They will.'

The man's laugh was harsh. 'What's the catch, nurse? People don't give nobody sump'n for nothin'.'

Miss Russell smiled at him. 'Oh yes they do – quite often. You'd be surprised. Try it and see.'

The man's face softened. 'Gee, nurse, that's swell!' He turned and called over his shoulder. 'Hey, Fanny! The boy's goin' to have them shoes! What you know about that?' He turned back to Sue. 'Come in, Miss Barton,' he urged. 'I guess you'll think it's funny I kep' you standin' in the hall – but I was sore. I know you done a lot for my wife – but it seemed to me like you just made trouble an' got our hopes up for nothin'. So I wasn't goin' to let you take care of Fanny no more. Come in! Come in!'

Miss Russell watched while Sue did the dressing, gave the patient a bath, and made the bed. It wasn't until they were on their way downstairs that Miss Russell said quietly, 'Miss Barton – is that man at home most of the time?'

'Why, yes. He's out of work, you know. What –'

'He's an able-bodied man, intelligent and responsible. Is there some special reason why he shouldn't take care of his wife, leaving only the dressing for you?'

Sue was startled. 'No,' she said. 'I – I guess I didn't think about it. I wanted to make the woman as comfortable as I could. And I'm so sorry for them. It seemed – sort of – nice to do all I possibly could – and make them feel that somebody took an interest in them.'

'I know, my dear. I've felt the same way, very often. But you're here to teach them how to take care of themselves. You spent an hour doing work that he could have done – and which you had much better be doing for someone who is alone and helpless.'

'I see. Thank you,' said the crestfallen Sue.

They went on, trudging through narrow streets, picking their way among children and dogs. Sue wondered how long it would be before everyone in the district knew her, as they knew Mrs Kirmayer. It would be gorgeous to have one's own district – but she'd have to learn a great deal first. And she mustn't make any more mistakes like the last one.

'What's your next case?' Miss Russell asked.

Sue hesitated, wondering if she had been stupid here, too. Then she said, 'The case is supposed to be a new baby, born at home – but I think the real case is the mother. I don't know what to do about her.'

'What's the trouble?'

Sue dodged a whizzing boy on roller skates, and stepped over a basket of dried herring. Her forehead puckered in a frown.

'It's an odd situation,' she said. 'The woman is young – only twenty. Her name is Crasniki – she's Polish – and it seems that her mother insisted on her marrying a man of fifty – who offered the best price for her. He was about to leave for America, to make his fortune – the way they all do, you know. The poor girl scarcely knew him, and she didn't like him very much, anyway. But here she is, married to him, and in a strange country – and with a baby. She doesn't speak much English, but I can understand her, after a fashion.'

'Is her husband good to her?'

'Why, yes. He's kind and all that. But they're awfully poor. And she doesn't seem to care about anything.'

'I shouldn't think she would!'

'I know. I can't get her interested, even in arranging the apartment. She could easily have curtains in the windows, and a geranium in a pot. But she won't bother. I mean – she hasn't ever bothered. Now, of course, she's in bed – and she just lies there, without the slightest interest in anything.'

'Does she still dislike her husband?'

'I don't think she pays much attention to him.'

'Is she fond of the baby?'

'Oh, yes. But it's only a week old. She hasn't got used to it yet.'

'Well,' Miss Russell said slowly, 'I can tell you better what to do when I've seen her.'

They found the patient in bed – an inert lump. Her blue eyes were dull, and her mouse-coloured hair hung in tails around her face. The baby slept beside her.

She roused slightly when Sue and Miss Russell came into the bare little room, and she seemed grateful for the care Sue gave her, but she made no effort to talk. The room was dusty, and the few pieces of furniture stood about crookedly with no attempt at arrangement. Old pieces of sheeting, unhemmed, hung at the windows.

While Sue made Mrs Crasniki comfortable and bathed the baby, Miss Russell dusted and straightened the room. But she said nothing which gave Sue any help in the present problem.

After they left the house Sue waited hopefully for suggestions, and as none came she said a little timidly, 'Do – do you think there's anything that can be done about her?'

'Oh! I'm sorry, Miss Barton. I didn't mean to keep you in suspense – I was thinking. There's a great deal that can be done with that situation. It should be quite simple to change Mrs Crasniki from a miserable little lump to a normal, gay young woman – and the room from its present condition to one of reasonable charm.'

'Oh, goodness!' Sue gasped. 'I – what should I – you mean –'

Miss Russell laughed. 'Oh, it's not as difficult as all that. It's quite simple. Do you want me to tell you what to do, or would you rather work it out yourself?'

It was several moments before Sue replied, and had Kit been present she could have told Miss Russell that when Sue's lips set like that she meant business. Sue said, at last, 'I'd rather work it out myself, if you don't mind. At least, I'd like to try to do it. If I don't seem to have much luck I'll come and ask you.'

'That's fine! I thought you'd want to do it yourself.'

Miss Russell returned to the office shortly after this, leaving Sue to finish her visits alone, and trudge on through the worn old streets and up and down the shaky staircase, trying to figure out what to do for Mrs Crasniki that would produce such miraculous results.

'I don't,' she thought, 'even know what it is she needs. But I'll find out if it takes me six months to do it.'

6
'Frien's'

The maddening thing about Mrs Crasniki's situation was Miss Russell's insistence that it was all very simple. Sue didn't find it simple at all.

As soon as Mrs Crasniki was out of bed Sue tried to interest her in taking walks, in reading Polish novels borrowed from the library, and in making curtains for the apartment. Mrs Crasniki sat apathetically, nursing the baby and saying nothing.

Sue tried something else. If Mrs Crasniki had a pram for the baby she'd almost *have* to go out, and once in the thronging streets she'd be bound to take an interest in life. There were really good secondhand prams for as low as five dollars. Why not buy her one?

Mrs Crasniki accepted the pram. She even seemed pleased, and she went out with the baby immediately – as far as the doorstep, where she sat rocking the pram back and forth in the thin winter sunlight, and stared at nothing.

Sue was at her wit's end.

'But I *won't* run to Miss Russell – yet,' she promised herself. 'There must be some way –' She turned aside into one of the tiny parks that dot the East Side, and sat down on a bench in a sheltered corner.

'What's the matter with me?' she wondered. 'I've tried – and worried – and schemed – but nothing works. What is it she ought to have?'

Something an interne at the hospital had said came back to Sue now. The remark had concerned the arrangement of pillows, to ease a patient's aching muscles after an operation. 'Try,' the young doctor said, 'to think yourself into the patient's body. Try to imagine yourself lying in the same position with a cut in just that place. If you can do that, you'll find that your own muscles, responding to the imagined condition, will tell you where pillows are needed.'

Surely, Sue thought, the same principle would apply to a mental ache. It was just a question of *feeling* it. What was it like to be Mrs Crasniki – to be only twenty and losing one's prettiness – to be in a strange country without friends?

Friends?

Sue sprang to her feet. That was it, of course! Mrs Crasniki ought to know some lively woman – she ought to have a little fun! 'Why, she's bored to death – that's what's the trouble,' Sue thought. 'If I could find just the right person – some jolly, kind woman – only there aren't many Polish people near by.' But there must be dozens of good-hearted women near by. The nationality wouldn't matter, for the poor had such a great capacity for kindness to one another. Sue laughed aloud, suddenly. Why not just walk along the street and pick one up?

She slung her bag over her arm, dodged through the traffic on Allen Street, and turned up Grand, to branch off into the little streets with their barrow markets – Ludlow – Hester – Orchard. Sue walked on slowly, looking into the faces of the women as she passed. There were many friendly faces – and far more happy faces than she had ever seen in Fifth

Avenue. There were Jewish faces with a haunted look behind their laughter. There were Scandinavian faces, broad and placid, with high cheekbones. There were Italian faces with bright dark eyes. There were quick Irish faces. But as yet no face that was right for Mrs Crasniki – no face which had the right amount of both vitality and understanding.

Orchard Street was as densely packed as Coney Island on a hot summer's day. Sue was edging her way through the crowd when a massive arm reached across in front of her, seized a boy by the shoulder, and removed him from Sue's path as though he were a baby.

'Letta th' nurse to pass, Arnoldo *mia!*' said a hearty Italian voice.

Sue turned and looked into deep-set, intelligent eyes, shining with friendliness. White teeth flashed in an energetic smile, and a pair of enormous hoop earrings of heavy gold quivered in the sun.

Sue stopped short. *This* was the face she had been seeking – a warm, maternal face, vital with friendliness.

'Oh!' she cried involuntarily.

'Whatsa matter? You looka for me?'

'Yes,' Sue replied simply. 'I was looking for you. I want to talk to you – if I may.'

'Oh, sure! Sure! Come disa way. I help you, maybe?'

The broad figure lunged through the crowd to a doorway, and turned to Sue with lively curiosity.

'*Ecco!* You tella me whatsa matter!' The woman's vitality was like a strong, clean wind.

Sue laughed. 'I'm going to – but I'd like to know your name first.'

'You looka for me – dunno my name! Da's funny!'
The huge bulk shook with delight at the joke.

'It was your face –' Sue began, momentarily at a
loss.

'Eh? Well, my face, she named Maria Bencordo.
What you mean – I do it. For a blue nurse – anyt'ing.'

'Oh, thank you, Mrs Bencordo! You see, there's a
little Polish girl –' She recounted the story of Mrs
Crasniki, omitting nothing – describing the situation,
the condition of the apartment, the girl's apathy. 'So
you see,' she finished, 'I thought if I could find her
some friend who would understand – if she could have
a little fun –'

Mrs Bencordo's earrings shook with sympathy.
'Aw,' she said. 'Da poor leetle one. Looka – for
young girls da good time it maka pretty lika flower. I
fix dat easy. She gotta baby. *Allora!* I gotta ten. I
know whatta momma likes. Nize words for da
bambino – yes? You taka me, now. I maka frien's.'
She turned and screamed into the crowd. '*Tony!* Tony
– you watcha de leetle ones for Momma!'

A black-haired boy with his mother's laughing eyes
darted through the crowd, nodded, and disappeared.

'A good boy – Tony,' said his mother. 'Now come.'

Mrs Crasniki was still sitting on the steps, still
jigging the baby's pram back and forth – her wispy
figure slumped in dejection.

'*Si!*' Mrs Bencordo's earrings quivered. 'Da
povera! Looka, nurse – you waita here. I go – maka
like I happen by.'

The vast figure went forward, moving strongly and
steadily, and approached the pram with a broad
smile.

Sue, unable to resist the temptation to listen, stepped into an adjacent doorway.

'Eh!' she heard. 'Whatta nize baby – so pretty! A fine baby! Boy – maybe?' She bent over the pram, her earrings flashing.

Mrs Crasniki stirred and looked up, her eyes lighting faintly in response. She nodded assent.

'So!' Said Mrs Bencordo, with approval. 'A son! A leetle man – to maka beeg an' strong for you! And sucha leetle, pretty momma!'

The simple flattering words were intelligible even to one with Mrs Crasniki's scant knowledge of English, and a latent spark of feminine vanity came to life in the form of a shy smile.

Mrs Bencordo beamed, hands on huge hips.

'Da's right! More smile now – uppa da corners! 'Whatsa matter, leetle momma? You seeck?'

Mrs Crasniki shrugged, her face suddenly impassive.

Mrs Bencordo nodded in complete understanding. Then she seated her enormous bulk on the steps beside Mrs Crasniki. 'Sure,' she said gently. 'I know – seecka here!' She touched her chest. 'Dat goes off bimeby. I know – me. An' w'en you got some frien's –'

'Frien's!' The tone dismissed the possibility.

'Sure! Frien's! Looka – to-morra some ladies come my house – for wine an' da cakes. You lika come – bringa da fine leetle son, huh?'

A tide of colour flooded Mrs Crasniki's pale face.

'Ladies?' she stammered. 'No, no!' She looked down at her dingy dress in an agony of embarrassment.

'Aw, now!' said Mrs Bencordo. 'Da dress? Is alla right! Me – I gotta no good dress. Da ladies gotta no good dress. We alla poor like old dogs. No money – no dress – on'y frien's. You come?'

Mrs Crasniki took a deep breath, and nodded timidly.

'Da's a good girl,' said Mrs Bencordo maternally, hoisting herself to her feet. 'To-morra I come getta you. No be afraid. Da ladies – dey gonna like you – sucha nize leetle momma, wid sucha fine son.'

She lumbered away at last, and Mrs Crasniki stared after her with dazed eyes. Once Mrs Bencordo paused, turned, and waved – a genial, intimate wave. Sue held her breath, and saw Mrs Crasniki's thin arm lift in daring response.

'You're a darling!' said Sue, coming up behind Mrs Bencordo. 'An absolute darling!' Her face was flushed with gratitude, and her eyes were warm, resting upon the kind, dark face before her.

'Aw!' said Mrs Bencordo, delighted. 'Me – I beena young an' scared, too, an' my man – he no understand. *E poi!* I lika your red head – an' I lika de leetle Crasniki, too. Dat's all.'

'I still think you're a darling!'

Mrs Bencordo's teeth flashed in a wide smile. '*E una bontà in lei, anche!*'

'What does that mean?'

'It say – you are a good girl – good!'

They smiled at one another.

Sue continued on her round of visits in a glow of relief and satisfaction, but it was several days before she had a chance to see Mrs Crasniki again, and when at last she climbed the long stairs to the little

apartment the door was opened by a startling appari-
tion – Mrs Crasniki, bristling with curlpapers.

The room was immaculate. So was the baby. There
were gay curtains at the windows. The bed was doing
duty as a couch, and was bright with pillows. A scarlet
geranium flamed in a pot on the table.

Mrs Crasniki, only partly dressed, was bustling and
preoccupied.

'What –?' Sue began.

'Ladies!' Mrs Crasniki explained. 'Come to-day!'

'Oh!' Sue cried. 'How nice! And the room is lovely!
Where did you get that pretty material?'

'Huh?'

Sue pointed to the curtains and sofa cushions.

Mrs Crasniki spoke proudly through a rustling of
curlpapers. 'Mrs Bencordo – give,' she said. 'My
frien', Mrs Bencordo!'

Sue swallowed. 'I'm so glad! And now you're
having a party! Is – is your husband pleased?'

There was no shrug this time. '*Ja!* He like.' She
glanced at the geraniums. 'Frum him,' she said. 'He
say – I – I gotta' – the inflection was exactly Mrs
Bencordo's – 'I gotta make pretty for sucha nize
lady-frien's.'

And the last thing that Sue heard as she closed the
door on her way downstairs was, 'My frien', Mrs
Bencordo.'

7
The Step on the Stairs

Shortly after Mrs Crasniki's rejuvenation some very odd things happened in the little house. Sue and Kit had gone to bed early one night – Kit was back in her own room now – when they heard the usual faint brushing sound that preceded the familiar scream – but the scream itself was an utter failure. It *began*, this time, with the hideous, whispering sigh, gave a hoarse squawk, and ceased abruptly.

There was an instant of silence. Then, from both rooms simultaneously, came shrieks of laughter.

'*Sue!*' Kit called. 'Listen to it, will you! It's got a *cold*, or something!'

'More likely it's ruptured its vocal cords, screaming.' Sue sprang out of bed and went to the head of the stairs, just in time to meet the Step. She laughed again, 'right,' as Kit said, 'in its face,' and called over her shoulder, 'it's still able to be up and around. Do you think if I fixed up an aspirin gargle, and left it on the stairs, the ghost would take it? I could write out directions.' She giggled.

'Why not put out a bottle of iodine for it?'

'Well, that would be all right, too.'

Sue returned to bed, still laughing, but a little later something occurred which was far from amusing. She woke up, thirsty, and pattered across the landing to the bathroom. Then, irritatingly wide-awake, she

turned on her light and began to read. Ten minutes or
so later she sat up in bed, startled and sniffing. There
was gas leaking somewhere – growing stronger every
minute.

Sue got up quickly, slipped on her bathrobe, and
went to Kit's door.

'Kitten!' she hissed. 'Wake up – quick!'

'Er – uh – what?'

'It's me – get up! There's gas coming from somewhere!'

Kit scrambled out of bed, thoroughly alarmed.
They put on all the lights, and ran downstairs to
the kitchen. Every jet on the stove was tightly
closed.

But the kitchen reeked with gas.

The girls sprang to the windows and flung them
open, letting in the cold night air.

The smell of gas lessened slowly, became a faint
sourness, and vanished. Kit lighted a match and
tested the burners. There was no trace of any leak.

The girls stared at one another with frightened
eyes.

'My gosh!' Kit whispered. 'What's going on around
here? Wha – what's it trying to do – kill us?'

Sue's grin was very feeble. 'I – wouldn't know. It
hasn't confided in me. Come on upstairs!'

Back in Sue's room, Kit said slowly, 'Well, if it's
trying to kill us it isn't very bright about it. You can't
asphyxiate people when they're sleeping in a room
with all the windows wide open.'

'That's so! But what *is* the idea, then?'

'Search me. Maybe you made it sore, laughing at it
on the stairs. What do you think we'd better do?'

'Let's wait a while – say an hour – and then come down and test the burners again.'

They did so, but on the second testing the match burned here and there among the slim pipes without a flicker. And there was no smell of gas; so they returned to bed convinced that the whole episode had been merely a freakish and unaccountable accident.

The following evening, when they came home at their usual time, Kit opened the front door and fell back, choking, as a wave of gas enveloped her.

Both girls dashed down the steps into the street, filled their lungs to bursting with fresh air, and, holding their breath, rushed into the house and flung open the windows – the doors – the French windows opening on the garden. While the air cleared they hung out of the windows.

'Well,' said Sue, 'I guess this is the end of our original theory that the ghost is trying to murder us – because what would be the point of filling the house with gas when we aren't in it?'

'Let's call the gas company.'

The gasman found nothing wrong.

'There ain't no leaks here,' he said, disgusted, and, gathering up his tools, departed, leaving the girls furious, once more, with the ghost.

Later, over the dinner table in the little restaurant around the corner, Sue said, rather crossly, 'I'm sick of all this business. Let's do something about it.'

'Got any ideas?'

'Well, sort of. I think we ought to begin with the steps, first, and see if that leads us to anything. You know the way they don't come up when there's anybody on the stairs –'

'Yes, but what –'

'*I* think it's because having us there is dangerous for it. I don't know why, but I'd like to see if I can find out anything more – and I thought – suppose I crept half-way down the stairs, oh, quite a long while before anything usually happens – and just sat there, and waited?'

'Mercy, Sue! What if it closes a nice, cold, invisible hand on your neck?'

'Or throws a blanket of gas over my head, I suppose. Then you can save me. Can you imitate my voice?'

'For Pete's sake! Why – I guess so. I can try.' She tried, and produced a very fair imitation of Sue's voice.

'Not bad,' said Sue blandly. 'Now I'll tell you my idea. You'll have to be pretty athletic – but it'll be worth it – I hope. About ten o'clock we'll get ready for bed, and make a lot of noise doing it – baths and things. Then I'll sneak down the stairs and wait. I can see perfectly with all that light from the electric sign. You go in my room and call out good-night – in my voice.'

'And then, I suppose, I make a leap for my room, and answer you – is that it?'

'That's it. You certainly do catch on, dear!'

'What you really want is a nice elderly kangaroo who has spent the best years of his life developing his leap. I'm going to have a wonderful time bawling out, and galloping, and bawling some more – while you sit comfortably on the stairs.'

Sue grinned. 'Yes – ringside seat. Only you're not supposed to gallop. You just kind of waft across, very silently.'

'Can I breathe?'

'I don't see any particular point in it, but of course if you're going to be obstinate –'

'Not at all. I just thought it would be easier.'

'So – taking the line of least resistance! You probably have criminal tendencies. Do you find that things go all blank every once in a while?'

'Why, yes, I do – every time I close my eyes. It's the strangest thing! How did you ever guess?'

'Oh, I have ways of knowing. How about our paying the bill and getting back to our muttons – or should I say gas?'

Kit closed her eyes and gave a faint gasp.

'Oh, dear!' she said. 'I guess you'll have to pay the bill. Everything's gone blank again. I can't even see.'

'All right – you win, this time. I'm the goat.'

The girls had a rule, instigated long ago by Connie, that whoever got the worst of an argument must be the 'goat' no matter what the occasion. Sue paid the bill without a murmur, and they walked home, arm in arm.

The evening dragged interminably. They talked, read, manicured their nails, talked again, and Kit, seized with an impulse to tease, related a horrible tale of a murder which had been committed in the woods of Nova Scotia, near her own home. Sue instantly capped it with the once notorious, but now almost forgotten story of the axe murderers on the Isles of Shoals, off the New Hampshire coast. She embellished it with a few details of her own, reducing both herself and Kit to a state bordering on panic.

'Are we idiots!' Kit said as they put out the living-room lights and went upstairs. 'I hope you have nightmares!' She took second turn at the bathroom, and before she was out of the tub Sue had crept down the stairs and was sitting, huddled in her bathrobe, half-way down. Her feet, in soft felt slippers, rested on the ninth stair.

'You remind me,' said Kit, addressing the hall, 'of the woman you just told me about, sitting on those rocks, waiting for the murderer to find her.'

Sue gulped.

Kit ran about chattering, first in her own voice, then in an imitation of Sue's.

She was doing a good job, too, Sue thought, listening from her perch on the stairs. But what a sell if the ghost didn't come to-night!

The house gradually became quiet. Kit's light went out. Sue waited, motionless, straining her ears. Once or twice it seemed to her that there was movement somewhere, but she felt it rather than heard it. Then, so close behind that cold chills ran down her back, she heard the brushing sound, followed immediately by the scream. It was an unusually harsh scream, unusually prolonged.

Kit's feet thumped on the floor, carefully noisy, and a moment later Sue had another chill. The fifth stair from the bottom began to creak! She peered down, her muscles stiffening involuntarily. The step came up, slow, deliberate, unmistakable – and Sue had a sudden, desperate longing to stand up and run; but she clenched her hands and sat quiet. She could see the treads stir slightly – the seventh, the eighth – Sue held her breath. Her feet – the toes curling with tension – were still on the ninth stair.

And the ninth stair – *lifted!*

She was not mistaken. Her feet were on the tread when it pressed upward – very slightly, but very certainly upward. Five minutes dragged by. There was no further sound; no movement. Sue waited another five minutes. Then she raised one hand high above her head, where it could be seen by Kit, who responded at once with a general sound of tramping and voices.

Under cover of this noise Sue tiptoed back up the stairs and went into her room. Kit followed.

When the door was closed Sue turned with sparkling, triumphant eyes.

'That's no ghost.'

'*What happened?*' Kit was breathless with suspense.

'There's somebody in the cellar!'

'In the – but how could –'

'Kitten, those steps are made by somebody pushing the treads of the stairs – *from underneath*!'

'NO.'

'Yes. You don't realize it when you're just looking at them. The stairs creak, and you see that they move just a tiny bit. But I had my feet on the ninth stair, and I felt it being pushed up!'

'Great snakes! What about the scream?'

'I – don't know yet. But that brushing sound was in the wall.'

Kit sat down on the bed and looked at Sue incredulously. 'Are you making all this up? Because how could somebody be in the wall?'

'I don't know.'

'What'll we do?'

'I suppose we ought to look in the cellar, but I'm

not very crazy about it. We don't know who's there, or –'

'And what about the gas? I don't like that, Sue.'

'Neither do I, but I don't seem to feel any urge towards the cellar.'

'What's the good of all this, then? After all, you started it. I thought you were going to be intrepid.'

'Not at all,' said Sue hastily. 'I only wanted to do a little detecting. I don't want any hand-to-hand battles.'

'I wouldn't mind a battle,' Kit said slowly. 'I mean, if you're sure the ghost is just a person – and he hasn't got a gun. I'm pretty hefty – and I'll bet I could swing a chair with anybody.'

'Oh, *no*! Don't be an idiot!'

'Why not – I mean – well, anyway, if you don't want to go down to the cellar, why couldn't we hide behind the living-room couch for a while, and see if anything happens? If he's going to do anything with the gas he has to do it in the kitchen – and we'd see him. If we knew what kind of person he is, we'd know what to do next.'

'But Kit – the cellar door is locked.'

'Maybe he gets in some other way that we don't know about. For all we know he may have a key to the front door.'

'*That's* a comforting thought! Besides, if he's in the house now, he'd hear us creaking down the stairs.'

'They won't creak if we're careful to step close to the wall, and right on top of the nails. I learned that trick when I was a kid – from my brother.'

'Don't they ever creak, that way?'

'Sometimes,' Kit admitted. 'You have to try them

out, first, keeping count, and then, when you go down, only step on the safe ones.'

They experimented successfully with the stairs, and then went back to Sue's room, to wait until the intruder should think them asleep. At the end of half an hour they crept down again, silently, in their stocking feet, and crept across the living-room floor to the couch. It stood a little out from the wall, and the girls moved it a trifle further, so that they could sit behind it.

They waited a long time, growing stiff and cramped. The living-room was full of shadows and the girls' eyes ached with staring at them, and at the dim rectangle that was the door to the cellar. The room was growing colder, too, and little whispering draughts wandered over the floor. Something tapped suddenly on a back window, and the girls started – but it was only a twig on the little tree in the garden.

The couch was low-backed, and by stretching upward the girls could see over the top without difficulty. Sue stared around the room until it wavered before her. What was the use of sitting here? They were catching nothing but colds. Sue leaned towards Kit, to suggest returning to bed, but before she could speak Kit nudged her sharply. Sue's heart gave a painful leap.

Kit had ducked down and was now peering cautiously around her end of the couch. Sue peered around her own end.

There was a thin black line up one side of the cellar door!

It widened slowly and a draught moved from it across the floor and under the couch. The cellar door had been hooked when they went upstairs, and now it was opening, slowly and stealthily, revealing the yawning blackness of the cellar.

Something detached itself from that blackness – a grey shadow – moving swiftly into the deeper shadows of the kitchen.

Kit rose quietly to her feet, and before Sue realized her intention had picked up a small, straight-backed chair and reached the kitchen door in two strides. Sue darted after her on silent feet. The chair swung upwards in the same moment that Kit's other hand found the wall switch.

There was a sharp gasp and, in the dazzle of light, a movement of recoil – by the stove.

The chair came slowly down, to rest on one leg on the floor.

'For – Pete's – sake!' Kit said.

Sue stared, speechless, over Kit's shoulder, at a tousled, hard-eyed figure backed against the wall.

'He – he's a *girl*!' The voice was Kit's.

The girl's lips twisted. She spoke out of the corner of her mouth.

'So what?' And then, as neither Kit nor Sue replied: 'Okay! You got me ! Go on an' call the cops! I don't care!'

It was that childish 'I don't care' which told Sue how frightened the girl was. She couldn't be more than seventeen or eighteen, Sue thought.

After an instant of silence Kit said, 'What do you want?'

'None of your business!'

'But it *is* our business. This is our house. What are you doing in it?'

'What's it to you?'

'Quite a lot,' Kit said reasonably.

'Sez you!' It was a snarl. 'Go on an' call the cops!'

Sue found her voice. 'We don't want to call any cops,' she said gently. 'We aren't going to do anything to you at all. Really! Come out in the other room and sit down – maybe we can straighten this out.'

'Oh, yeah? What is this, anyway?'

Sue laughed. 'What do you think it is?'

'I dunno. A loony-bin, I guess. Whadda yer keepin' me here for, if yer ain't goin' to call the cops?'

'Because,' said Sue, with a quick, disarming smile, 'you've made awful monkeys of us – and we'd like to hear how you did it. Won't you tell us – please? We'll let you go right away, afterwards. I promise!' She looked very charming, standing there, the light gleaming on her bronze-gold hair and her eyes friendly and smiling.

Disbelief struggled with hope in the girl's eyes.

Sue held out her hand. 'Shake on it!' she said.

The girl hesitated, uncertain and puzzled. Then she extended a grimy hand with very black nails. Sue's slim white fingers closed warmly upon it.

'You – you ain't such a bad guy,' the girl said gruffly.

'Hey!' said Kit. 'I'm here too, and after all, I *didn't* hit you with the chair!'

'Poddon *me*!' the girl said with dignity, and held out her hand to Kit.

Sue, restraining her curiosity until they should have made the girl feel more at ease, suggested hot chocolate and sandwiches before they settled down to talk, and while these were in the process of making the girls had a chance to examine their visitor without appearing to do so.

She was sitting, with a swagger, on the chair which had been intended as a weapon against her. A stained, black beret was pulled down over untidy, wiry hair, which, if it had been clean, would have been golden brown. She wore a faded shawl, brown cotton skirt, and tennis shoes without stockings – in February. But she looked well fed. Her skin, under its sprinkling of freckles, was clear, and her wide mouth, with sensitive lips betraying the hardness of her eyes, had a good healthy colour.

Sue was stirring the chocolate. 'How old are you?' she asked suddenly.

'Eighteen.'

'Would you tell us your name? We have to call you something, you know.'

'You can call me Marianna if you wanter. It ain't my real name. My real name's Mary Ann Lawson, but I don't like the Mary Ann part, so I've decided my name's Marianna. It would make a good name on the flicks,' she finished complacently.

Sue's lips twitched, and Kit peered hastily into the ice box. Sue thought, 'Poor lamb! She's just a baby! *Flicks!*' Aloud, she said, 'The chocolate's ready. Let's go in the other room, and you can tell us how you worked the ghost.'

'It was like this –' Marianna began, when they were settled comfortably on the living-room couch. The story of her childhood was commonplace – and pitiful. Her mother had 'run off with another guy' when Marianna was a baby. Her father, a day labourer, had died two years before, and an aunt in

Brooklyn had grudgingly permitted Marianna to live with her.

'She was an old devil!' Marianna said. 'She put me to work an' she took every bean I made. She wouldn't let me go anywhere nor do nothin'. So last autumn I scrammed and come back to New York.'

Marianna had found work of sorts, washing dishes in a cheap Greenwich Village bar – for meagre wages and her meals. At night she got a bed in a municipal lodging house, or went to an all-night cinema.

'They're swell an' warm on a cold night,' she said. 'An' you can wake up any time, an' there's the pitcha goin' on.'

It was at this point that the story ceased to be commonplace, for on a night in the autumn Marianna had discovered the little brick house. There were no curtains at the windows and the house was dark, so she had gone up the steps and looked in. The house was furnished, but obviously untenanted, and the happy thought came to her that there was a splendid warm place to sleep, free, for a few nights – if she could get in. She tried the windows without success, and at last went round to the back – by way of the next block of houses and several fences – to see if she could get in through the cellar.

'Them winders was barred too,' she said, her voice quivering with the bitter frustration of that moment. 'But then I seen pipes comin' in from next door. There was a cellar winder open over there, an' it wasn't barred. There was people in the house, too, but I shinnied over the fence in the dark an' went in by the winder. I thought there'd be a door into the cellar of this house – but there wasn't.' She paused.

'How *did* you get in?' Kit said.

Marianna grinned. 'I was pushin' around the other cellar, an' I come up against a loose board in the partition between. You could push it out some, at the bottom. So there I was!'

She had slept comfortably in what was now Sue's bed, for several nights, slipping out at daybreak through the adjoining cellar. 'I busted the lock on the winder over there,' she explained. 'But it didn't show, so nobody done nothin' to fix it.' Then, one night, she found her house full of workmen's tools, paint pots, and stepladders. It was being decorated for new tenants.

'That gimme a lousy jolt,' she said. 'I guess I'd got to thinking the house belonged to me. An' it was so nice an' warm, an' all. I din' know what to do, but I hadda do sump'n quick.'

So she went to the cinema – and there she saw a picture in which there was a haunted house. There were screams and footsteps. This seemed a perfect solution for her. People would be frightened out of the house, and it would be hers for the winter. No way of accomplishing this occurred to her, however, until, as she was crossing the street, a police car went by, with the siren on.

The result had been a hurried visit to a toy shop in the Village, where she had calmly shoplifted a toy siren which worked by pulling a string.

Sue and Kit swallowed this frank confession of theft without a word, concealing their shock.

Marianna had returned to the little house and examined it carefully. The plasterers had stripped the hall to the lathes, upstairs and down. It was possible to attach the siren behind the lathes, dropping the string down behind the cellar stairs.

'The boards was pretty solid against the wall,' Marianna said. 'But I poked a hole through with a chisel outa the workmen's things. The string come through, with some pokin', in the cellarway, an' I pushed it behind that long beam, side of the cellar stairs. That way, see, I could just stand in the cellar an' pull the string. Boy! How she screeched!' She slapped her knee, laughing raucously. 'Gee,' she went on, 'the very next day they plastered the wall and never seen it!'

The steps on the stairs had been simple. Marianna stood on the cellar stairs and pressed upward on the flight above with the palms of her hands, and as far as she could reach – which was to the ninth stair.

What most amazed the girls, however, was the shrewdness with which Marianna had thought out her plan of action. She had reasoned that people who are startled out of sleep or bed are easily confused and not very perceptive. So she always waited until the tenants of the house had gone to bed. Then she pulled on the siren once, briefly – so that it should not be traced to its location, and when she was sure that at least one person was on the landing, and 'scairt stiff,' she set the stairs creaking. The moment the last stair had done its duty, she ran quickly down the cellar steps – concrete steps which did not creak and on which tennis shoes made no sound – dodged through into the other cellar, and left the people in the house to worry.

'Oh, boy!' she said. 'I scairt out three lots of people – an' everything was fine – until you come!'

'But, I don't understand,' said the appalled Sue. 'Where were you when they had the police here?'

'In the other cellar.'

'But they must have known the cellars joined. Didn't they look over there?'

'Sure they did – but they didn't find me. The cellar over there is in two pieces.'

The girls looked bewildered.

Marianna explained patiently. 'Lookit,' she said. 'The front of that cellar is a furnace room, all neat an' nice. There's a wooden partition, with a padlocked door, that cuts it offa the back. The back is fulla junk an' stuff – and my loose board opens offa there. Quick as I made the steps on the stairs I'd hop back, pull the board tight after me, an' hide in the back part of the other cellar. The police looked in the furnace room, but the door in the partition was padlocked on their side so they never bothered to go through – an' if they'd come I'd a been outa the winder before they ever got to me. See?'

'Y–yes. But where did you sleep when there were people in *this* house?'

'Oh, there's some old sofa cushions in your cellar cupboard. I laid 'em on the other cellar floor an' slep' there.'

Kit said: 'That string, rubbing against the lathes, accounts for the brushing sound, doesn't it? But what happened the other night, Marianna? The siren didn't work.'

'Naw! The string caught on somethin'. You girls made me darned sore, laughin'. You wasn't scared, anyway, like the others was, an' when you got to laughin' I figured I might's well give up. Then I got mad. That's when I done that stunt with the gas. I – I didn't mean no real harm. I only turned it on for a minute or two. I thought sure it would scare you out – even if the other things didn't.'

'So *that* was it,' Kit said, a trifle grimly.

'How did you get up from the cellar?' Sue asked. 'I hooked that door myself.'

'That was a cinch – a little loop of wire. I could push it through the crack an' lift the hook out – an' lift it back after. I come in the house lots of evenin's when you was out. I seen all your things – books an' clothes an' all. An' I used to listen to you talkin'. You – you have a lot of fun, don't you? I – sometimes I thought – if only it wasn't for sleepin' on the floor, I'd kind of liked to let you stay. You was lots of company.'

Sue's eyes softened, but she said nothing.

'I'll tell you one thing,' Marianna went on. 'I couldn't never make out how you felt about the ghost. I was always listenin' – but I never heard a thing. You kinder had me stumped.'

'What are you going to do now?' Sue asked.

Marianna shrugged wearily. 'What's the dif?' she returned. 'I'll go back to the dosshouses – maybe – an' if I don't – it don't matter much.'

Sue ignored the touch of melodrama. 'Why don't you stay here for a few nights?' she said. 'We haven't a third bed, but this couch is really quite comfortable – and we've plenty of bedclothes.'

Marianna simply looked at her.

'How about it?' Sue urged. 'Stay a few nights, anyway. Maybe we can find some place for you to live – or get you a better job.'

'You – you mean,' Marianna said, 'that you want me to stay here – after all I done?'

'Of course!' Kit said. 'Why not? We don't blame you for that.'

Marianna hesitated, drawing a long breath. Then she said slowly: 'Gee – that would be swell. I – I'll stay – if you'll let me do some work for you. Maybe I could tidy up the house – or something.'

Sue was on the point of rejecting this offer. Marianna as a tidier didn't look promising. But she most certainly wouldn't stay unless she were allowed to do something – she was too independent to sponge. And she mustn't go wandering around the streets at night, or return to sleeping in those ghastly places. Something must be done for her. Sue glanced at Kit and received a brief nod.

'All right,' she said. 'It's a bargain. What time do you go to work?'

'Eight o'clock.'

'What time do you get through?'

'Around five.'

'Good! Whenever you can fit it in, you might tidy up, and sweep – and if you feel like it there are usually a few breakfast dishes. We take our other meals out.'

'Oh, sure,' Marianna agreed grandly. 'I can do all that with one hand tied behind me.'

Sue rose to her feet. 'That settles that, then. I'll get you some bedclothes. Have you got any pyjamas?'

'Gosh, no! You don't put on pyjamas to sleep on cellar floors.' Marianna giggled. 'You put on a overcoat – if you got one.'

Sue laughed – though she felt more like crying.

When she returned with the bedding Kit was in the kitchen and Marianna was carrying out the hot-chocolate cups. She turned to Sue, suddenly gruff.

'Say – how's chances on me havin' a bath?' Her face was a fiery red.

'Why, of course!' said Sue, who had missed neither the painful gruffness nor the flush. 'Go right up. I'll give you some towels.'

Marianna departed with alacrity.

Sue found her towels and pyjamas, and passed them through the bathroom door. Then she returned to the kitchen.

'Well, old thing,' she said to Kit, 'we seem to have taken a Henry Street problem right into our hearth and home.'

'I should say we had! My goodness, Sue! We'll have lots of chance to practise applied psychology – and habit forming. But Sue, she's an awfully smart kid. Imagine figuring all that out. It's a pity she hasn't had a decent chance.'

'Yes, it is. Shall we – let her stay on with us – for a while, anyway?'

'Oh, yes, Sue. We can't do anything else, really. I mean – what she needs is some kind of a home – and while this isn't exactly a *Little Woman* act – still, it's not so bad. Only I hope she hasn't got the light-fingered habit. My hair simply curled on my head when she sprung that casual little bit about shop-lifting.'

'I think she's all right,' said Sue. 'Underneath, I mean. And she's so gruff and prickly that I've a hunch she's hiding a soft spot.'

'Yes – I had the same hunch. We ought to be getting to bed, Sue. It's after twelve. We'll be dead to-morrow.'

'I know, but we'll have to wait until Marianna's out

of the bathroom. Kit – do you suppose she'd be offended if we offered her some clothes?'

'I don't know. She's awfully sort of standoffish. Maybe we'd better wait a day or so, until she get to know us better.'

The girls put out the lights, except the one over the couch, and went upstairs, thankful that the ghost, as such, was gone for ever.

A little later Marianna emerged, rosy from her bath. The removal of several layers of grime revealed a fresh, highly intelligent young face, on which habitual sullenness had not yet left any permanent mark. She had washed her hair, and was dressed in Sue's pyjamas.

'Gee!' she said. 'I feel swell.'

'I'm glad,' Kit said. 'And your bed is all ready and turned down. I hope you have a good rest.'

'Thanks, kid,' said Marianna.

8
Interlude

Marianna kept the house neat and the dishes washed, getting up in the darkness of the winter mornings to sweep with such vigour that the girls feared for the rugs. She clattered among the pots and pans in the kitchen, running water in the sink until it sounded like a waterfall. She breezed through the rooms with the effect of a March wind.

'Heavens!' murmured Sue, listening to the sounds below. 'You wouldn't think anybody could dust so distinctly, would you?'

Marianna's work was near by, and in the evenings she reached home before the girls, to make the beds and straighten the upstairs rooms. The girls saw little of her, however. She seemed anxious not to intrude, and when they remained at home she nearly always made some excuse to go out.

Sue and Kit were still going to the little reataurant for dinner, and sometimes they invited Marianna to postpone her evening meal and come with them. Sometimes, though rarely, she accepted, always insisting on paying for her own dinner.

These occasions were a strain. It was difficult not to be embarrassed by the company, in public of a large, athletic-looking girl who presented the general appearance of a stranded barge woman, who talked out of the corner of her mouth in tones that could be heard a mile away, and who ate jucily, her elbows on the table, her napkin on the floor and any finger handy doing duty as a toothpick.

'Gosh!' Kit said, after one of these episodes. 'What a cosy little meal! Honestly, Sue, there *can't* be any need of her being so appalling. I believe she does it on purpose.'

'She does and she doesn't,' said Sue, dropping into the only comfortable chair in her bedroom.

'That's enlightening – and thanks for the nice seat,' said Kit caustically.

'Sit on the bed, then. It's fairly solid. No, but I mean, I think she feels horribly uncomfortable. She realizes that she doesn't know how to act, so she puts up a great big bluff of not caring – and behaves all the worse – the poor kid!'

'I suppose that's it. I do wish she'd let us give her some decent clothes. She doesn't make enough money to buy any.'

'Well, she won't let us. But I like that in her, Kit. She's got a lot of pride, even if it is misguided.'

'That's all very well, but she'd feel a lot better if she were nicely dressed – any girl would. And maybe she'd try to live up to the clothes.'

'That's a thought! Let's see – what would we do if she turned up on our call slips, as a case? Because that's what she is, really. And there's no law that says a Henry Street nurse can't practise what she teaches. Come on, now – what would *you* do?'

Kit pondered. 'Well,' she said after a moment, 'I should say the thing to do was to approach her along lines that she would understand. That's what we're taught to do on the district. Miss Firrell says people will accept almost any suggestion if you use the right tactics.'

'Yes – and that always sounds simpler than it is. What kind of tactics would you use on Marianna?'

'The kind she uses herself – sledge-hammer tactics. How would this do –?' Kit talked at some length, and Sue listened, grinning.

'Let's try it!' she exclaimed, when Kit had finished.

They waylaid Marianna the following night, and announced bluntly that they thought she ought to let them give her some new clothes.

Marianna's chin stiffened.

'So that's what *you* think, is it?' she said. 'Try an' do it!'

'That's awfully unfair of you, Marianna,' Kit said.

'Huh?'

'She's right, Marianna,' Sue put in. 'It *isn't* fair of you. It – it's lousy of you, in fact.'

'Why?'

Kit rose abruptly from the living-room couch. 'Because,' she said with assumed indignation, 'it's darned mean to slap people in the face when they're trying to be friends.'

'Yes,' said Sue. 'You do all kinds of things for us that you don't need to do – and we let you. But when we want to do something for you, you stick out as many bristles as a porcupine!' She glared at Marianna, who glared back, bewildered.

'Lissen –' Marianna began.

Kit interrupted her promptly. 'You certainly do bristle, Marianna! Did it ever occur to you that it isn't generous *never* to accept, when you give all the time? Anybody'd think a gift from us was poison!'

'And,' Sue added, 'it's rotten to keep us under obligations to you all the time. You act like a – a – bully – always trying to be on top.'

'That's exactly it!' Kit cried. 'Anybody'd think you hated us – and it makes us feel awful!'

Marianna drew a deep breath, looking from one stern young face to the other. There was a long silence, in which the girls' schemes visibly hung in the balance.

'Gee!' Marianna said at last. 'I – I never thought of it that way. I – guess I been a – oh, heck! Trot out your darned clothes. I'll take 'em!' It was the nearest approach to an apology of which she was capable.

Triumphant, the girls ran upstairs to search among their things – for a dress and coat and shoes.

Marianna took the bundle with an almost meek grunt and disappeared into the bathroom. She was gone a long time, but the door opened at last, and she came slowly down the stairs, her face flushed but grim.

'*Marianna!*' the girls cried in chorus, staring at her.

They were sincerely startled, for Marianna in well-cut, becoming clothes was a very different person from the shapeless, untidy girl of an hour ago. The smoky blue of Sue's dress brought out the unexpected lights in Marianna's hair, now neatly combed back from her face. Kit's second-best coat, with its smart shoulder lines and flaring collar, gave her a surprising dignity of carriage, and transformed her usual sullen expression into one of aloof pride.

'Yummy!' Kit said. 'You – you look like something from old Russia. I'd no idea my coat had such possibilities!'

'And look what that dress does to her eyes and hair!' Sue cried. 'You're stunning, Marianna!'

'Thanks,' Marianna said gruffly, but her eyes shone.

They bought her a hat the next day – a hat which Sue claimed she had not worn as it was not becoming to her. As this was the liberal truth – Sue having brought the hat home in a box – she had no qualms of conscience. But the girls didn't dare to press their advantage. Further improvements could wait, except for the question of a job for Marianna. She mustn't go on washing dishes in that bar.

'We'll find her something, sooner or later,' Kit said. 'There's no use in worrying. We have to do enough of that all day, in the district.'

February was nearing its end, and the girls were beginning to feel settled at Henry Street. The daily routine was no longer broken by lectures, and though the girls had enjoyed them, and benefited by them, it was pleasant to be able to plan the day's work without having to allow for time out – except the weekly afternoon off. This, the girls spent at the Craigs', telling the round-eyed Eleanor stories of their work.

As the days went by they found that the dozens of flights of stairs they must climb daily had ceased to make their legs ache. Their bags no longer seemed so heavy on their arms – in fact, they forgot that they carried bags, so accustomed were they to the habitual weight.

The mornings were the busiest part of the day, for urgent cases were always first on the list. These were the accidents, the pneumonias, the contagious diseases, and Sue became more skilful every day in

doing complicated nursing with no facilities except
her bag, her young strength, and her enthusiasm. She
learned when and how to call ambulances, and came
to know their drivers and internes. She learned how
to approach hostile members of a family by persuasive-
ness and tact. She learned to contrive and improvise –
to make bassinets out of arm-chairs, trays from
bread-boards, a shower bath from a large kerosene
can with a tube attached to the spout and a washtub
for the bather to stand in. She was informed by a
serious Italian wife that the best and most certain way
to stimulate a patient's appetite was to put a poultice
on his stomach – a poultice made by frying bread and
olive oil, soaking it in wine, and rolling it in cinna-
mon. She gave baths and made beds and did treat-
ments. She learned to hold her tongue and keep her
temper with rude landlords. She learned to relax at
lunch time, so that she could set out again, refreshed.

The afternoons were not as busy, except during
sporadic outbreaks of influenza, and it was then that
she had time to make friends in odd ways and in odd
places. She found that road sweepers are kindly souls
who know all that happens in the houses along their
streets. They often stopped her as she passed, to tell
her of someone who was ill and in need of help. A
policeman waylaid her to ask about a diet for himself.
A postman wanted pamphlets on the care of young
children, for his sister on Staten Island. A gentle old
rabbi hurried after her on the street and pressed a
ten-dollar bill into her hand, 'to help any of my people
who are in need.' Once she found her way blocked by
a huge crowd celebrating an Italian wedding. Bottles
were hurtling out of windows and fights taking place

indiscriminately. Sue was unable to extricate herself from the crowd until six grinning young policemen surrounded her, and paraded her to safety through the cheering mob.

She wrote enthusiastic accounts of Henry Street to her father and mother, and to Bill. Bill replied warmly, saying that all this would be invaluable when they were married. 'Not that I'm marrying you for your profession,' he added, 'but it will come in handy.' He inquired about Connie, asking when and where she and Phil were to be married. If the wedding wasn't too far away he might be able to come up for it.

Sue was thrilled. She would see Bill again! They might even announce their engagement, just before the wedding. But no – the wedding was Connie's special time. The announcement of the engagement could come afterwards. This year, she thought with a happy sigh, was going to be gorgeous!

Connie wrote to them regularly every week, her amusing, characteristic letters reminding them only too vividly of those days in the hospital when they had been three instead of two – when, united, they had gone from one scrape to another. Those scrapes – though the girls didn't suspect it – had furnished some astonishing new legends to the famous old hospital from which they graduated. But Connie was lost to all that now. She was through with nursing – preferring marriage to any other career. Her last letter had come from Baltimore, where she was visiting friends. She wrote gaily, as always. Phil, her fiancé, was well. No, the exact date of the wedding hadn't been fixed. She'd let them know later. She and Phil had decided to go straight home to their little house and not bother with a honeymoon.

'That's too bad,' Kit said, reading the letter. 'Here's Connie with a million dollars – and they can't have a honeymoon.'

'She didn't say they couldn't. She said they wouldn't. It might be that Phil can't afford it and won't take Connie's money – but it's more likely that they don't want to bother.'

March came and went in a series of warm, pleasant days. The East Side broke out in a rash of window boxes. Small boys played marbles on the pavements. Hopscotch designs covered the streets, and the late afternoons were filled with the beat of skipping ropes and the voices of little girls, counting. It was in March that Sue found a job for Marianna, as checker in a mail-order house.

'What the heck is a checker?' Marianna demanded, when informed of her opportunity to become one.

'Why – er – when orders come in they're filled, and then somebody has to check over the goods, with the order. That's all. The pay is better than you're getting now, and the hours are better, too.' Sue refrained from mentioning that the surroundings, also, would be a great improvement over those found in a Greenwich Village bar. So Marianna became a checker, and presently the girls noticed that she had ceased to talk out of the corner of her mouth, and their hopes for her rose. Marianna, however, seemed to have decided that she had improved enough, and the next suggestion proffered by the girls fell very flat indeed.

She had been spending more evenings at home of late, listening with interest to the girls' talk, and asking occasional questions about their work at

Henry Street. So, one rainy night when they were all three sitting around the living-room fire, Sue led up to the subject of education, progressed from that to a little talk on the excellence of New York's night schools, and finally suggested, with what she felt was great tact, that it would be nice for Marianna if she attended evening classes.

Marianna heard her out in silence.

'Naw,' she drawled, when Sue had finished. 'I ain't goin' to no school – see? If anybody don't like me dumb they can lump me.'

The girls exchanged a despairing glance.

'We like you a lot, Marianna,' Sue said gently. 'We'd like you whether you had an education or not. And we aren't trying to push you around. We just thought –'

'Yeah – but I think different. I guess you mean all right, an' you been swell to me – but I ain't goin' to no school. I ain't had no trouble gettin' a job, without a education, so what the heck!'

And that was the end of the discussion – if it could be termed a discussion.

In April there was a severe storm. Snow fell for three days, and was followed by freezing weather. The magnolias in Central Park turned black. Window boxes vanished indoors. Small boys continued to play marbles – in grimy slush – but the little girls and their skipping ropes were no longer in evidence.

It was during the worst of the cold wave that Sue had a very strange experience.

She returned to the office one afternoon to find one of the nurses greatly upset. A mental case, who was going to have a baby, had jumped out of a fifth-storey window just before the nurse's arrival.

Sue had had a hard day, and the story, with all its gruesome details, took a deep hold on her imagination. It haunted her dreams that night, and she woke in the morning feeling depressed and apprehensive. Her apprehension increased when she learned that her first visit that morning was to a young Scotchwoman who was going to have a baby.

Sue realized that her forebodings were absolutely groundless, but they persisted in spite of reason. She found the house without difficulty. The apartment was on the *fifth floor!*

'Don't be silly!' she told herself firmly, outside the door.

She tried the bell, but it didn't work. All seemed oddly silent, and Sue was immeasurably relieved when, in response to her knock, a woman's voice with a thick Scotch burr said, 'Come in!'

Sue turned the knob and found the door locked.

'Mrs MacCrae!' she called. 'Will you unlock the door, please? It's the nurse from Henry Street.'

The only reply was a burst of maniacal laughter. Sue's heart began to pound and she shook the door calling out again, 'Unlock the door, please, Mrs McCrae!'

The laughter continued, shocking and horrible.

Sue turned and dashed down the stairs in search of the caretaker. She found him in the basement.

'Oh, please!' she gasped. 'Come – quickly! There's something awfully wrong in the McCrae apartment. Mrs McCrae won't let me in – and she's laughing – awfully.'

'That ain't Mrs McCrae,' said the caretaker, unmoved. 'That's the sister. She's stayin' with the children. Mrs McCrae went to the hospital this morning.

'*Never mind!* Something awful is happening. Hurry!'

Her alarm was contagious and when she ran back up the stairs the man was close behind her. There was no sound from the apartment now, but the door was still locked. The caretaker banged on the door and rattled the knob. There was no reply.

'Break the lock,' Sue urged. 'Quick!'

The caretaker set his shoulder against the door and lunged. After two efforts it gave way and they rushed into the room.

It was empty!

'Oh!' Sue moaned. She and the caretaker searched the four rooms and found nobody. But there were no open windows and Sue began to hope.

The living-room was a pleasant place, with one corner filled with potted ferns and a rubber plant. Sue returned there presently and her breath stopped when, from behind the ferns, came a sudden chuckle. Then the Scotch voice remarked briskly, 'Gude bye. Come again!'

Sue and the caretaker reached the spot together and beheld, looking at them with bright, knowing eyes – an enormous green parrot in a cage.

'Hello!' the parrot said affably.

'Well – I'll be –' said the caretaker. His face was still white.

Sue laughed shakily. '*Naughty* Polly!' she said to the parrot.

The parrot laughed, hiccupped, laughed again. 'Oh!' it shrieked, delighted. 'Oh! Oh! Ha, ha, ha!'

The strange half-human sound followed Sue and the caretaker down the stairs.

Afterwards, turning the matter over in her mind, Sue reflected that this was the first experience she had had which even remotely approached the popular idea of a Henry Street nurse's life.

'According to the newspapers and magazines,' she complained to Kit, 'we go around in pitch darkness, even if it's broad day – stifling our sobs – and using our haloes to light up dungeons.'

'I know. People don't seem to understand that we're not undertakers – but the happy ending. They've no idea that delightful things, and funny things ever happen to us. Take yesterday. I stopped to speak to a barrow man, to ask how his wife was doing. She was one of my patients. He said, 'Vait!' and rushed off before I could stop him. And there we were – the barrow and I – all alone. People came up and wanted to buy things, and there didn't seem to be anything to do but sell them. You should have seen me, very Henry Street, and complete with bag, doling out oranges and bananas and giving change – until that ridiculous little man came back with his wife in tow, so I could see her for myself. If I ever get fired from Henry Street I'm going to buy a barrow and set up in business.'

9
A Minute and a Half

Sue returned to the office one afternoon to go home with Kit, and, finding her in the lower hall in conversation with a social worker, wandered about idly, waiting.

There seemed to be an unusual amount of flurry going on somewhere in the distance. There was running to and fro, and a steady hum of voices, but Sue, thinking that there was a meeting of some kind, paid no attention to it.

She wandered upstairs, drifted into the main living-room, and found herself standing before a large oil painting – a copy of one by the famous artist, Moroni, which hangs to-day in the Louvre, in Paris. It was a simple and beautiful portrait of a tailor bending over his cutting table – an Old World figure, full of dignity, his face tranquil and absorbed.

There was a story connected with the picture. Some years ago, before Miss Wald had retired from active charge of Henry Street, she discovered that some of the young people in the neighbourhood were developing an unpleasant snobbery. Many of them were the sons and daughters of tailors, and were, it seemed, ashamed of their fathers' occupation.

Miss Wald brought the portrait of the tailor to the Henry Street House, where she hung it conspicuously in the living-room – so that the youngsters might know that the world honours a fine craftsman, whatever his work may be.

Sue stared up at the absorbed face of the tailor, her own warm with sympathy, wondering what he would think to-day of this new world in which young people learn to laugh at old customs and sneer at things which are good and beautiful.

She heard a step behind her, but did not turn until a quiet voice remarked:

'You seem interested in the tailor.'

Sue turned then.

Close behind her stood a woman of middle height, with greying hair and a strong, rugged face – the kindest face that Sue had ever seen, but yet a face of power and determination. The room was electric with her presence.

Sue didn't reply immediately. She felt startled and oddly uncertain. Then she glanced at the tailor and said slowly, 'Yes. I – I am interested in him. I think it's a lovely picture – but I think the reason it's here is lovelier.' She paused, wondering if she ought to explain, but the woman seemed to know the story, for she nodded briefly. 'It seems to me,' Sue went on, 'that the reason it's here is – is sort of typical of the whole spirit of Henry Street.'

'Do you? Why?'

Sue groped for words. Ordinarily she was glib enough, taking refuge when moved in the flippancy of her generation. But there was something in that kind face which made pretences impossible. She said awkwardly, 'Because – there's a togetherness in Henry Street. I – I mean – here nobody is better than anybody else – no one kind of work is more elevated

than another. And everybody tries to make things –
right – for everybody else.' She stopped.

'Yes – go on.'

'Well, you see – if it were possible for Henry Street
to expand – I mean, over the whole world – after a
while there wouldn't be any more poverty – and
snobbishness. The – the more you think about it – the
bigger it gets.'

The woman smiled, and it was as if sunlight had
fallen suddenly upon her face.

'It's nice to hear that,' she said. 'Do all my nurses
feel that way?'

'Certainly they do! I –' Sue broke off with a gasp.
The quiet voice had said 'my nurses.' Sue's tongue felt
stiff and she swallowed. '*Oh*!' she cried. 'You're not –
are you – I mean, you couldn't be – *Miss Wald*?'

'Yes – I'm Lillian Wald.' It was said, not in the
manner of one making an announcement, but with a
kind of humility, as if the admitted importance
attached to the name were an accident of circum-
stance surprising to Miss Wald herself.

Sue's own name became ridiculous and without
meaning.

'I'm Sue Barton,' she said. It was an apology.

'I'm glad to have met you, Sue Barton – and may I
wish you long happiness in your work?'

'Th–thank you, Miss Wald,' Sue stammered, and
winked back sudden tears.

When Miss Wald had gone Sue remained standing
motionless beneath the picture of the tailor. Kit found
her there.

'Oh, here you are! I've been looking everywhere
for you! Sue! What do you think – Miss Wald has been
here! I mean – Miss Wald in person!'

'I know. I saw her.'

'*You* did! Where?'

'Right here, a few minutes ago. She talked to me.'

'Gosh, Sue! How marvellous! What did you feel like? Is she nice?'

'I felt,' said Sue slowly, 'like taking off my hat, and putting it on the floor and crawling under it.'

'For Pete sake! Why?'

Sue steadied her voice with an effort. 'Because – she's a great lady, Kit. I don't – mean – because she's important and famous – I mean – she's a great lady – *inside*.'

Kit stared in astonishment. 'Whee!' she said. 'How could you tell? I mean, if you didn't know who she was, would you have thought she was different from anybody else?'

'I didn't – and she was. I felt it the minute she came into the room. She has a kind of power – but it's more than that – it's a – a kindness – in her face, in her voice, in her eyes. And you feel that she couldn't possibly be petty, or small. She's the first person I ever met in my life that I *know* couldn't do a mean thing!'

'Heavens! How long did you talk to her?'

'About a minute and a half.'

'You mean to say that you collected all that in a minute and a half.'

'You don't collect it,' said Sue quietly. 'It hits you like a ton of bricks.'

10
Changes

In May, Miss Pettigrew, the anxious nurse, left Henry Street.

No one was surprised, for Miss Pettigrew had had hysterics twice in the office – once because she had misplaced a record, and once because it was necessary to tell a woman with seventy-five canaries that they were the cause of her asthma and must be disposed of.

The lost record was not important, and the matter of the canaries, though unfortunate, was not a major problem. But Miss Pettigrew was determined to find life as hard as possible – an attitude which is anything but helpful to a Henry Street nurse, or her patients.

And so, one morning, a new student took Miss Pettigrew's place, and the worried little nurse vanished from Henry Street. There was a rumour that Miss MacDonald had found her an excellent hospital position, where her talent for worry would have less scope.

Sue was genuinely sorry, but she couldn't help feeling a little proud of her ability to judge character, and, remembering the jaunty nurse with the hat, thought that there was another who wouldn't last. Henry Street was definitely *not* the place for the whoops-my-dear type.

In June the nurses changed to lightweight summer coats of navy blue, and the black felt hats were

replaced with cool straw. Lower Manhattan was
enchanting in June. The mist that hung over the
harbour lay upon the narrow East Side streets and
little parks in a thin blue haze, and the sunlight,
streaming through the Elevated structures to the
shaded street below, made a gay, marching pattern of
stripes along the cobblestones. Window boxes were
out again, splashing the scarlet and yellow across the
grey faces of the tenements, and chronic invalids
stirred from their winter lethargy to sun themselves
on street corners and park benches.

Along the East River the big boys became daring
and incredibly Spartan in ragged bathing trunks –
keeping a watchful eye out for the police; for swim-
ming in the polluted waters of the East River was
forbidden. Their shouts and splashings echoed up the
narrow streets, and little boys forgot their games, to
gaze in awe. Little girls were dignified and matronly,
wheeling perambulators in the parks, or herding half
a dozen younger children across some main traffic
artery, where the acrid breath of passing cars was hot
on bare little legs.

Sue, passing with her bag, watched these non-
chalant sallies into danger and was appalled. The
existence of children in the slums seemed to be
entirely a matter of the survival of the quickest.

It was in June that Connie wrote, saying that she
and Phil were to be married in New York, on August
nineteenth, at the Little Church round the Corner.

Sue wrote to Bill at once, and when his reply came,
saying that he was to be Phil's best man, she put on
her hat and coat and went for a long, joyous walk –
though she had been walking all day.

She knew just how Bill would look at the wedding – tall and distinguished, his clear blue eyes steady, as always, and his firm lips curved in a little, serious smile. Afterwards, they would go somewhere together and talk about their work, and their plans, and each other, and when he had gone back to New Hampshire she would have it all to remember – until next time.

So life went on a little more gaily than usual because of the undercurrent of special happiness and anticipation. The soft June days slipped away until, suddenly, it was July.

The city became an oven, and the nurses trudged over pavements that burned through the soles of their shoes. Their hats left red marks on their foreheads, and there were damp streaks across their sleeves – made by leather straps pressing upon hot arms.

The tenements held the heat unbearably, so that during the day families lived in the street, where there was at least a breath of wind from the river. At night they slept in the parks or on fire escapes – but their sick lay panting in the heavy stale air of the tenements, waiting for the hour when the nurse should come to relieve their discomfort for a little.

Sue lost all count of the days and of the number of people she sent to rest cures in the mountains, or the country, or to the seashore. She sent innumerable pale children to camps, and was made glad by the sight of them, later, brown and vigorous.

Both she and Kit worked all over the Centre, sometimes in one district, sometimes in another – wherever one of the nurses needed help, or was on holiday, or ill. They had difficulties and disappointments. There were obstinate old people, still heads of their families, who refused to accept new ideas. There were greedy landlords who had no mercy on wretched tenants who were behind with the rent. There were men, posing as doctors from the Health Department, who fleeced the gullible poor of their last penny. These men were afraid of the Henry Street nurses and spread unpleasant propaganda about them.

But there were more ups than downs, and the girls were happy – though they longed for the day when they would have their very own district, when they could walk along the street and say, 'I belong to this. These people are mine.'

At night they straggled homeward to baths and dinner and lazy evenings in the little garden, where the baking earth gave up its heat when the sun went down, and the evening breeze, though sooty, cooled their faces.

Marianna brought them iced drinks there, and remained to talk or listen. She seemed fascinated by the girls' work at Henry Street and was never tired of their stories. Her gruff manner was always carefully in evidence, but her voice had toned down and her vocabulary increased – both in unconscious imitation of the girls, who noted the change and rejoiced, though they didn't dare mention the fact to Marianna. Nor did they venture so much as to breathe the words 'night school.'

It seemed to the girls, now, that they had always been in New York. The city was as familiar as the contents of their bags. They loved the slim towers, shining in the sun or hidden in low clouds; they loved the blue canyons of the streets, the lavish shops, the theatres, the breezy water front where squat ferries churned and tugs hurried and great liners swung in and out with the tide.

But towards the end of July Sue's contentment was shaken to its very roots – by a letter from Bill.

I've just heard from Phil Saunders [he wrote], arranging the details of the wedding. And I regret to inform you, Miss Barton, that I am torn with envy. Why should he be marrying the girl of his dreams next month, while I stagnate in the company of a large, stiff-jointed Airedale? What sort of a world is this, anyway?

Sue, darling – let's drop this nonsense. I want to be with you. You say you want to be with me. All right, then, let's get married. Now! Right away! At once! I need you, and I've suddenly become old fashioned. Woman's place is with her menfolk – or anyway, your place is with me. Please, Miss Barton, marry me now. I do love you so much.

Sue's face was white. Still holding the open letter in her hand, she went out into the garden and sank down in one of the gay canvas deck chairs. She read the letter again, slowly and carefully. Then she stared, unseeing, at the cracks in the flagstone walk.

Kit joined her presently – a brisk Kit, who came out laughing at something Marianna had said, and whose laughter ceased abruptly at the sight of the motionless figure in the deck chair.

'Why, Bat!' Kit said. 'What's the matter?'

Sue didn't move. 'Everything!' she said in a dull voice.

Kit dropped into a chair. 'Do you feel like telling me?'

Sue looked up then. 'I do, if you wouldn't mind.'

'Don't be an idiot.'

'It's about Bill. I – I suppose you must have guessed we were engaged.' Kit nodded. 'I hadn't said anything – to anybody, because – because I hadn't. He agreed that I wasn't to marry him until I'd been on my own for a while – and now he's forgotten that, and wants me to marry him at once.'

Kit was silent for a moment. Then she said, 'You can hardly blame him for that, Sue. You've kept him dangling for an awful while.'

Sue shifted uncomfortably in her chair. 'I know – but he *promised*!'

'Yes, there's that. But still – don't you want to marry him, Sue?'

'Of course I do! I – I'm crazy about him! But, Kit – I can't just walk out on Henry Street before I've been there six months.'

'No, you can't. It's funny he doesn't see that. He always used to be a stickler for ethics.'

'Well, he doesn't seem to feel that girls have to be ethical. I haven't even had my own district yet, and I do owe something to Henry Street for all this training. Miss Russell said the other day that a nurse is more of a liability than an asset until she's been on the staff at least a year.'

'Yes. They don't bind us with a lot of contracts and agreements, but they do expect us to make some return for our training by staying on for at least a year and a half or two years. I don't see how you can do anything else.'

'That's just it – though it isn't all of it,' said honest Sue. 'I don't *want* to leave now. I'm marrying Bill for life – and this is my only chance to be on my own.' She paused, brooding. Then she said slowly, 'But I – I *think* I *would* leave, since he wants it so much, if it were just a question of my own feelings and his – because I have given him rather a miserable time. He's been awfully patient up to now.'

'Why don't you write and tell him you'll talk it over with him next month, when he comes up for the wedding? Time,' Kit said sagely, 'smooths out a lot of things. And when you're right there in front of him it'll be easier.'

'I'm not so sure,' said Sue, who knew Bill. 'And anyway there isn't as much time as all that – only about three weeks. But maybe when he's here he'll realize that Henry Street isn't just a Ladies' Sewing Circle.'

'Did he say that?'

'No – he did worse! He ignored Henry Street as if it weren't important enough to mention. It just doesn't exist as far as he's concerned.'

'Gee!' Kit said. 'Poor Bill! Honestly, Sue, it is awfully hard on him. He's waited for you for ages, and now when he never sees you, you can't blame him for being fed up.'

'I don't see *him*, either, and I hate it! But I couldn't help wanting a *little* life of my own, and now I'm started at Henry Street I don't think it's fair to run out on it.'

There seemed nothing more to be said. Sue wrote to Bill as Kit had suggested, saying that they could discuss the matter more easily when they saw each other. She raised no issues whatever.

Bill's reply was amiable, but confident. It was, in fact, too confident, and Sue's spirits sank still further. After all, she owed Bill something, too. She had promised to marry him, and here she was in New York, pursuing her own separate affairs. Bill had always been generous and sympathetic. Now he needed her she was trying to put him off again, and he was saying, though he probably didn't realize it, 'Choose between me and Henry Street.'

Perhaps she *ought* to leave Henry Street.

But no – she had obligations there, too, so no matter what she decided, it would be the wrong thing – unless Bill himself could be persuaded to change his mind, and do so willingly.

To make matters worse, Miss Russell called Sue aside a few mornings later, at the office.

'Miss MacDonald just telephoned,' Miss Russell began, with a somewhat rueful smile which made Sue uneasy. 'You know, of course, by this time, that you are going to be accepted at Henry Street. Your work has been splendid, especially on the Crasniki case. We're very proud of that, Miss Barton. It's made us appreciate how reliable you are – a person who can be counted on – and we shall be very glad to have you on the staff.' She paused.

Sue was torn between pleasure and misery. Henry Street felt it could count on her! But so did Bill!

'I'm afraid,' Miss Russell went on, 'that Henry Street is going to lose you. You're being transferred to Washington Heights.'

Sue tried not to believe her ears. It couldn't be that she was leaving Henry Centre – where she had actually talked to Miss Wald, herself. She couldn't be leaving the noisy, smelly, colourful streets, with their barrows and junk shops – leaving all her patients, and the friendly road sweepers and policemen, leaving Miss Russell for an unknown supervisor.

'You – you mean,' Sue faltered, 'that when I get my own district, it – it's going to be in *Washington Heights*?'

Miss Russell nodded sympathetically.

'I'm terribly sorry, Miss Barton. I'd hoped you would stay here with us. But one of the nurses at Washington Heights has had to resign because of poor health, so they're shorthanded – and you know we don't like to remove the nurses from their permanent districts. So we're very thankful to have someone to send them who hasn't a district, and will begin to be permanent *there*.'

It seemed to poor Sue that every other word Miss Russell had used had been the word 'permanent.'

'When – do I go?'

'You report to-morrow morning.'

11
Harlem

The Washington Heights office was in the Medical Centre, a big, new shining office, flooded with sunlight, and the nurses welcomed Sue – both as an individual and as a permanent staff nurse, though she had not yet officially become one.

Had she been sent to Washington Heights before Bill's letter came, she would not have noticed this very natural attitude on the part of the nurses; but now it stood out sharply, a continual reminder of her dilemma.

Miss Farrar, the supervisor, was a small, crisp person, with smooth dark hair, dark humorous eyes, and very beautiful hands. She was on excellent terms with her nurses, and there was a great deal of joking and laughter in the office.

'They have to see a lot that isn't pleasant,' she told Sue, 'and it's good for them to be able to come back here and behave like kids.'

Sue was in hearty agreement with this idea. 'I'm going to love it here,' she thought – and instantly felt guilty.

When she had been shown round and given a desk she sat down in the sunny main office and listened eagerly while Miss Farrar discussed the problems of the Centre, and of Sue's district – her own district, where she would be expected to make good.

She would have, Miss Farrar explained, a sprink-ling of Irish, Scotch, and Cubans, but most of her work would be among the black people on the West Side of Harlem – which included not only slums, but the rich Sugar Hill section where singers and dancers and orchestra leaders lived.

The chief problem in the slums was diet. The people ate the wrong kind of food, and the children had rickets. Something could be done about that, of course, but nothing could be done about overcrowd-ing in the tenements. Five or six families often shared one house, and as most of the grown people worked out by the day, the children were left alone, to roam the streets.

'Don't be discouraged if you make mistakes,' Miss Farrar concluded. 'It takes a long time for a nurse really to know her district, so that she can give the best of herself to it with confidence. But I'm here to help you. We'll all help you.'

They would, too, Sue thought miserably. And of *course* it took a long time – anybody ought to be able to see that – especially a *doctor*!

'Mrs Egan's district joins yours,' Miss Farrar was saying, 'and you'll relieve each other on afternoons off or when there's a rush. She's the best person to help you adjust and learn your way around, so I'm going to send you out with her to-day.'

Sue had not remembered any of the nurses' names, and had no idea which was Mrs Egan.

Miss Farrar, catching Sue's blank look, laughed. 'That's Mrs Egan over there,' she said. 'Next desk to yours.'

Sue turned quickly and encountered the amused

eyes of a slim, dark-haired girl, who winked at her.

Sue grinned in response and was turning to speak to Miss Farrar when the office door opened and the girl with the jaunty hat and whoops-my-dear manner walked in. Miss Farrar introduced her as Miss Glines. Miss Glines was casual, nodding at Sue and disappearing into the cloakroom.

A little later, when Sue and Mrs Egan were on their way out, Sue inquired tactfully about Miss Glines.

'She came when I did,' Sue explained. 'I noticed her in class and wondered what had become of her.'

Mrs Egan laughed. 'Yes,' she said, 'you do notice Glines. She looks as if she might take off from the ground at any minute – but she's one of the best nurses we have. Her patients are crazy about her – and she's a terrific worker.'

'I'm so *glad!*' Sue cried, impulsively. 'I – I thought –'

'Yes, so did all of us. But she isn't.'

The two girls walked on in a companionable silence for a time. Then Sue asked shyly, 'You – you are Mrs Egan, aren't you – not *Miss*?'

'That's right. Lots of the girls here get married, you known, and stay on. You – hate to give up the work, once you're in it.'

'Does – your husband mind?'

'Goodness, no! He thinks it's swell!'

And that, Sue thought bitterly, was a perfect solution – but it would never be hers. Once married to Bill, she'd be at least five hundred miles from New York, and about a million, as far as Bill was concerned, from Henry Street. But whatever Bill thought, he couldn't think away –

'Your district,' said Mrs Egan suddenly. 'Look – right over there!'

Sue gave a faint gulp, and Mrs Egan grinned understandingly.

The two girls were on the edge of a little park. Beyond it, bleak streets cut between stone, brick, and brown-stone tenements that sloped away downhill to a grey huddle of roofs, quivering in the July heat. It was a dreary aspect, but Sue looked upon it with instant affection and possessiveness.

Mrs Egan was watching her. 'You'll love working with the people here,' she said presently. 'They're so willing to co-operate, and so eager to learn. The lower East Side, where you've been, is a lot livelier – but after you've been here a while you wouldn't change for *anything*.'

'Oh, dear!' said Sue, involuntarily. 'I was afraid of that – I mean – shall we go on?'

They walked through the wind-swept streets, on which there were no white faces except their own. Mrs Egan stopped half a dozen times in a single street to inquire after husbands, or wives, or grandmothers, or babies, and each time bright eyes turned to her with complete confidence.

Her manner was quiet and unhurried – that of one human being to another. She was not there to exploit the people, or to be grandly feudal, but to help them stand on their own feet – and they knew it.

Their response was evident in their eyes, their voices, their gently courtesy, their eagerness to please.

The girls' first visit was to the young wife of a rich singer, living in a beautiful flat on Sugar Hill. Their

second was to a wretched family living in a coal cellar.
A young man, seeing them pass, dashed out to say
that his little Jeannie was sick, and would Miz' Egan
please call? She would. Enchanting babies caught at
her skirts as she passed. Small boys grinned up at her.
Little girls hurried to show proud gaps where a tooth
had been. All the children's clothes, even when
ragged, had been freshly washed and ironed. All the
rooms were clean – and Sue was inexpressibly proud,
for this was *her* district, and these were her people.

At Henry Centre she had felt, she now realized, a
little like a visitor, but here, because she had her own
district, she felt at home, and she looked forward
confidently to working by herself. Henry Street had
never seemed more important.

But under all the satisfaction – spoiling it – was her
worry about Bill. If she could only make him see!
Surely he would, after she'd talked to him. Because,
of course, he hadn't meant that about being old-
fashioned and thinking a woman's place was 'with her
menfolk' – as if she had no right to herself, and no
business to be a person. What he'd meant, under
cover of all that kidding, was that he was growing
more and more miserable. Oh, dear! Well, she would
make it up to him somehow.

Sue pulled herself up with a jerk and returned to an
awareness of littered streets, broiling sun, and the fact
that she was hungry. They had lunch in a little
cafeteria, supplemented it with long, cold lemonades,
and went on again.

Sue's respect for Mrs Egan increased as the day
wore on. Mrs Egan was no chatterer. If she had
anything to say she said it promptly, with no frills and

no drama. Behind her steady eyes and tranquil face her mind worked like lightning. Never for a moment did she lose her grasp on a situation or fail in tact. Hysterics subsided in her presence. Tall stories faltered before the twinkle in her eye. Childlike stubbornness melted into, 'Yas'm Miz' Egan, Ah'll do whatever you tells me.'

'Let's see that arm,' she would say, pushing her hat up off her forehead. Or, with a grin, 'You're making a sissy of that boy, Zeke. I don't care how pretty his curls are – you go and get his hair cut!'

Surely, Sue thought, an organization which developed girls into persons so real and fine, an organization which was doing work of lasting value, was not to be treated lightly – even by a man in love. He'd see that, once he was in New York.

The long shadows of late afternoon were blue over Harlem when Sue and Mrs Egan finished with the last case and set out for the office.

'Golly,' said Sue, wiping her damp forehead, 'this heat gets me down!'

Mrs Egan laughed. 'Oh, you'll get used to it,' she said. 'I nearly melted away, my first summer, but now I hardly notice the heat. After you've been here two or three years –' She broke off, staring ahead at a small green and white police car drawn up by the kerb. 'I believe that's Sergeant O'Day!' she exclaimed, pleased. 'I haven't seen him for ages! Come on and meet him. He's an old darling!'

As they approached the car a broad, kindly face under a crown of greying hair emerged from behind the wind-shield.

'Well! Well!' said a deep voice. 'Sure an' it's me gurl herself! How are ye?'

'Pining away for a sight of you. Sergeant, this is Miss Barton – and you'd better be nice to her or I shan't love you any more.

'Aw now, don't ye say that!' He turned to Sue, beaming. 'A redhead, is it!' he said. 'An' a pretty one at that! I'm pleased to meet ye, Miss Barton.' He held out a huge paw and enveloped Sue's hand.

'Then there is a chance for me?' said Sue, her face lighting with her quick smile. The Sergeant's eyes lighted in response.

'Aw now,' he boomed. 'A chancet? Why, 'tis sorry I am, this minute, that I'm no longer a lad.'

'You faithless wretch,' Mrs Egan cried. 'I thought *I* was your girl.'

'An' can I not have two?' the Sergeant demanded. 'Shure, an' I'll have to keep an eye on me young patrolmen afther this. Onless,' he added to Sue, 'ye've got some nice young feller waitin' on yer doorstep. I'll bet ye have, at that!' His delighted laughter shook the little car. 'Look at her,' he roared, 'givin' herself away wid the little face of her all pink!' He sobered. ''Tis a tough district ye got, Miss Barton, an' if ye need anny help don't forgit Sergeant O'Day's yer friend.'

Later, when the girls were on their way again, Mrs Egan said, 'He will be, too – and when Sergeant O'Day's behind you, the town is yours.'

This was more than encouraging, but in spite of herself Sue couldn't help thinking that here she was, starting to make friends at once, and to establish herself in this new district – which meant that it was going to absorb her, as usual.

'Oh, dear,' she said aloud, to Mrs Egan's bewilderment, 'everything's so difficult!'

12

Four, Fourteen, or Forty

The work in Harlem differed from that of Henry Centre, not in kind, but in need. On the lower East Side the people had been taught by the Henry Nurses for forty years, and their condition and understanding had improved immeasurably.

In Harlem the Washington Heights branch office had only been open since 1928, and the population had greatly increased since that time. People, still coming up from the South in swarms, crowded the tenements beyond capacity. The moment a family moved into a tenement the rent would go up – beyond what the family could pay. This was cruel and unnecessary, but the people were helpless, and their only solution was to crowd as many families as possible into one apartment. Knowing nothing of diet, sanitation, or child training, they needed instruction almost more than nursing care.

Sue, who was a born teacher, delighted in the work from the very first day, in spite of her worries about Bill and her regret at leaving Henry Centre. The people were fully aware of the value of what they were receiving, and no suggestion was too trivial to be acted upon, or too laborious to undertake. For in spite of their lack of knowledge, they had a tradition of cleanliness and were proud of it. Sue rarely found dirty rooms, even though the building itself might be in a shocking state of grime and disrepair. A room was seldom cluttered, even when it was crammed with treasured possessions. Each had its place, and no speck of dust lurked anywhere. The windows shone. The floors were swept. The bedding was spotless, and in almost every apartment Sue entered she found some member of the family washing or ironing.

Sue's uniform marked her instantly as trustworthy, with no axe to grind and no tricks up her sleeve. The people accepted her without question – as a friend.

The second day, when Sue went out alone, she had occasion to show a mother of six children how to plan a diet and how to budget the father's meagre earnings. The woman listened with anxious attention to everything that Sue told her. The children, meanwhile, were having their lunch, gathered around a pot of stew which was at the back of the stove. There were no forks or spoons in evidence. Brown little fingers dipped into the stew, poking about in it with happy unconcern, and six pairs of bright black eyes stared at Sue with unwavering interest – regardless of what was happening in the region of the pot.

'Do they always eat standing up?' Sue asked the mother.

'Why, yas, ma'am.' She seemed surprised at the question.

'Well, you know,' said Sue, with her friendly smile, 'it's bad for their digestions to eat standing up. They ought to sit at the table and have their own plates and knives and forks – and not touch each other's food with their fingers. If they learn to eat nicely now, like grown people, they won't be embarrassed later.'

'Thank you, ma'am. Yas, ma'am.'

Sue, not yet accustomed to Harlem, was uncertain as to how much the woman understood or intended to do, and so, the following day, she made an unexpected return visit, timing it for the lunch hour. What she found gave her a very clear idea of what working in Harlem would be like.

The one table in the room, which yesterday had been bare and unused, was now spread with clean newspapers. Around it, on boxes, sat the six youngsters, each with a bowl of corn-meal mush and a spoon. They were drinking milk from individual pickle jars. The father, home for his noon meal, was waiting on the table.

'Oh!' Sue cried. 'This is splendid! It's exactly what I meant.'

The mother's teeth flashed. 'Thank you ma'am,' she said. 'We's a-tryin'.'

The man turned to Sue. 'We-all is thankful to you,' he said with gentle dignity. 'We *wants* our kids to grow up right.'

That same afternoon Sue had another example of this readiness to be taught. Mrs Egan, who was rushed that day, had asked Sue to call on one of her patients, a woman who was expecting a baby any day.

'Just see how she's getting on, will you?' Mrs Egan said. 'I simply haven't got a minute.'

Sue found the patient in bed, though with no immediate signs of the baby's coming. The one-room apartment was partitioned off with sheets, so that the bed was screened from the view of the seven-year-old child playing in the doorway. The flat top of the sewing-machine was spread with newspapers for the nurse's bag. The chest of drawers had been cleared for the doctor's instruments, and the clothing for the expected baby was folded and ready under the pillow.

Sue was touched. There was something at once pitiful and fine in this desperate reaching up for better ways of living and doing.

'I'm so glad I was sent to Washington Heights,' she thought. 'I'll do all I can to help them – in every way I can. If Bill knew what this work was like he'd feel the same way! He – he'd be crazy about it! And if he could see the children –!'

The problem of child training was a serious one in Harlem, for much of it was left to youngsters of fourteen and fifteen, who tended small brothers and sisters while the parents were away at work.

It is not difficult to teach a worried mother the principles of habit forming in children, but it is quite another matter to teach a girl, herself still a child, how to be patient and understanding with strenuous smaller children. Sue found herself in difficulties with just this situation before she had been a week on the district.

She was sent to give general care to a little girl who was confined to her bed with a broken leg in a heavy cast. The case, at first sight, presented no unusual features. Little Mary was docile, and required only the usual bath and bedmaking, and massage. There were two other children, Effie, aged fourteen, and Alonzo, a handsome youngster of four. Both parents were away all day, leaving the younger children in the care of Effie, who, during Sue's first visit, seemed amiable enough.

Alonzo, however, was sucking his thumb, and Sue took up the matter with Effie. 'We'll give him a star chart,' she said. 'I'll show you how it works.'

Sue rummated in her bag for paper and pencil and a small cardboard box.

'Look, Alonzo,' she said presently, and held out her hand. On her open palm lay several small gold stars.

'Wha' dat?' demanded Alonzo, his round angelic little face alight with interest. His hair was not kinky, but softly curling, and he rumpled it with a chubby hand as he peered at the glittering stars.

'They're gold stars – for you. See!' Sue drew a design of squares on the paper, seven across and four down. 'There,' she said. 'This is to-day's square. This is to-morrow's. For every day you don't suck your thumb Effie will put a gold star on the square for that day. And if' – Sue paused dramatically – 'if you have a whole week of seven stars, *then* you get a great big one.'

Alonzo stared up at her incredulously, thumb in mouth.

'Don't you want a star for to-day?'

The curly head bobbed vigorously.

'Then you must take your thumb out of your mouth.'

The thumb was hastily withdrawn.

'That's splendid. Isn't he a good boy, Effie?'

Effie made no reply, and Sue mistook her silence for reticence.

When Alonzo's attention was elsewhere Sue tried to explain to Effie. 'You must praise him when he's good. There's no fun in doing the thing you don't want to do unless it's made worth-while. You have to learn to want to do it, and then, after a while, it gets to be a habit.'

'Yas'm,' said Effie with indifference.

On Sue's next visit, however, Effie was anything but indifferent. 'He's bad, Alonzo is,' she said, almost in tears. 'And Maw says Ah got to take keer of him. Ah cain't do nothin' with him, Miss Barton. He hits Mary on her bad leg an' he won't mind, an' if Ah don' give in to him, he has a temper tantrum.'

Sue explained – clearly, she thought.

'You can change naughty ways to good ones,' she said. 'I expect Alonzo is jealous because Mary has had so much attention since she's been sick. The way to stop that is to have Alonzo do little things for Mary, and praise him when he does. Make him feel important and responsible. If he has a tantrum don't fuss with him, or let him find that it gets him anything at all. Just put him in a room by himself and leave him there alone.'

Effie's face was sullen. 'Ah'll try, Miss Barton. But Ah wisht –' She paused and glared at the cherubic Alonzo.

'Did he get a star for to-day?' Sue asked, changing the subject. 'Let's see your chart, Alonzo.'

The boy's eyes rolled at Effie and his lips quivered.

'Ah done took it away frum him, Miss Barton,' Effie said. 'He was gittin' the paper all dirty. So he had a nawful tantrum.'

Sue marshalled all her patience. 'Did you do what I said?'

'Oh, yas. Ah done lock him in the coal cellar all afternoon. It wukked fine. I got to play out in the street for long whiles. I got a frien' with roller skates. She let me take one.'

Before Sue could find a suitable comment to these revelations Mary piped up from the bed.

'Effie,' she announced with relish, 'tole Alonzo to git me a drink of water or she'd clip him one, an' Alonzo got mad an' throwed water all over her Effie,' she added, 'done stayed out all afternoon, and I'se all alone – on account Alonzo, he was in de coal cellar. Maw, she was a-goin' to lick Effie, but she tole her you said to do all dat.'

Here was a fine mess. There must be some way of getting Effie to understand, but explanations were of no use – in view of Effie's genius for misconstruing.

'That wasn't just what I meant,' said Sue at last. 'I'll show you. Only, first, we might give Alonzo his chart. It doesn't matter if he gets it dirty. It's his.' She turned to Mary. 'Did he suck his thumb yesterday, Mary?'

'No'm, he din't. He tried real hard not to.'

Sue smiled down on the gratified Alonzo. 'That's fine, Alonzo,' she said. 'Come on, now, and we'll put on the star.'

While Sue was making Mary's bed she tried a little demonstration for Effie's benefit.

'Alonzo,' she said, 'would you help me a minute? See, just put your arm under Mary's head while I turn the pillow. That's the boy! That's splendid! My, you're strong, aren't you!'

Alonzo's dark little face expanded in a wide smile. 'I'se a big boy,' he said proudly.

'You certainly are. I'm going to tell your mother how you helped me with Mary.'

Alonzo ducked his head and his thumb went into his mouth. He snatched it away instantly and looked up for approval. Sue gave it to him with good measure. Then she handed him the small waste bag. 'Would you take this out in the kitchen for me, Alonzo?'

He strutted away, carrying the bag carefully with both hands, and Sue turned to Effie. 'That's the way I meant you to do, Effie. I didn't mean you to scold him or smack him. And you mustn't put him in the coal cellar and lock him in. Just put him in the kitchen and shut the door – and do it quietly and quickly. The idea is to surprise him out of his tantrum, and then leave him by himself – just until he's calmed down.'

'Yas'm,' said Effie reluctantly, seeing her pleasant afternoons in the street vanishing almost before they had begun.

When Alonzo returned he was carrying a small alarm clock, holding it happily against his ear, and before Sue realized what was happening Effie sprang forward with a shriek.

'Bad boy! You leave that be!' The palm of her small hand caught Alonzo across the cheek with a resounding crack. 'Ah'll *surprise* you-all!' she shouted.

The ensuing tantrum was a masterpiece of its kind.

Alonzo, with piercing screams, hurled everything at Effie that he could reach or lift, including a glass and saucer from Mary's bedside table. Then he flung himself wildly to the floor, kicking, and tearing at his own hair.

'That's how he is!' Effie yelled above the din.

Sue, whose sympathies were entirely with Alonzo, took one step forward, picked up the yelling child regardless of his flying heels, and carried him to the kitchen, closing the door behind her as she came out.

'There,' she said. 'He'll be quiet in a few minutes. And when he comes out I want you to see what I do.'

'Yas'm, Miss Barton.' Effie's voice was stark with boredom.

Sue was in despair. If this continued Alonzo would rapidly become a serious problem – and through no real fault of his own. As for Effie – 'Goodness!' Sue thought. 'What an idiot I am! What an absolute fool! It's Effie who needs her habits changed. But how? If Effie were only young enough for a star chart . . . well . . . why not? An older edition of a star chart – Sue drew a deep breath of relief.

'Effie!' she said.

'Ma'am?'

'How would you like a beautiful new pair of roller skates, all your own?'

'Oo! Mah lan's, Miss Barton! Ah raikin Ah'd just about go outer mah haid!' Effie's eyes bulged at the prospect.

'Well – if you will do just what I say about Alonzo for one whole month, I'll give you a pair of roller skates!'

'Oh, Ah will, Miss Barton! Ah shore will!'

'All right, now listen carefully. You aren't to strike Alonzo, or speak to him in a cross voice. Leave him his star chart and make no fuss if he sucks his thumb. Act as if it didn't matter. Only – if he doesn't, he gets a star. And make him feel important about doing things for Mary – the way I just did. Don't give him orders. Don't tell him he's bad. He isn't bad. You've seen what to do about the tantrum. I'll show you the rest in a minute.'

'*Yas, ma'am!*'

'Remember, the whole idea is this. Alonzo will be good if he finds it's pleasant to be good and that it's not a bit of fun to be naughty. So pay lots of attention to him when he's good, and *none* when he's bad – no matter what he does – even if he has a tantrum. Just put him in the other room, as if you didn't care. Do you understand?'

'Yas indeedy!'

She did, too, Sue thought – the little scamp! Maybe it was a bad idea to bribe the child, but if Effie once, by whatever means, learned to manage Alonzo properly, she'd keep it up – both from habit and because she would have an easier time.

The yells from the kitchen were subsiding and after a while Sue rose and opened the door. A small, tear-stained figure straggled out.

'Hello, Alonzo.' Sue's voice was casual. 'I was just going to show Mary a game. Would you like to play?'

Alonzo nodded tearfully. He seemed dazed by the indifference of his reception, and looked at Effie.

She crossed the room to him with the confidence of one who already felt upon her feet the glory of new skates.

'Come now,' she said, in exact imitation of Sue's tone. 'Sit yere on the bed. Ah'll bet you can beat at this game.'

Sue repressed a grin. It didn't make much difference, after all, whether you were four, fourteen, or forty – luring yourself into reasonable behaviour was always simplified if there was a star chart in the offing.

13

'Anny Way Ye Look at It –'

Three weeks is not a long time, but it was sufficient to give Sue a gradual change of perspective in regard to Bill. She began to think she had been hasty in jumping to the conclusion that he regarded her work as of no importance. Actually, he had said nothing about it – nor did he in following letters. Besides, why worry until he came? She had enough to do without that. And so, little by little, as the days went by, her natural optimism asserted itself, convincing her that everything would come out all right.

The morning hour in the office was always pleasant. The nurses talked and laughed, and teased Miss Farrar with a happy freedom from restraint. Once Miss Farrar had said in mock-tragic tones that nobody ever, ever paid any attention to her. The nurses grinned and said that she was so small they couldn't see her. But the remark started a train of thought in somebody's head, and on the following morning the nurses filed up to the desk, one by one, with great solemnity, and presented Miss Farrar, each, with a small gift.

'For dear Teacher,' they said, as the pile of bundles and boxes rose higher and higher. There was candy, and fruit, and chewing gum. There were Mickey Mouse lollypops, animal crackers, and bottles of pop. There were even a box of strawberries and a hard-boiled egg.

Miss Farrar, when she had recovered from her surprise, was caustic in her comments, but the nurses knew that she was pleased. Sue guessed that she was also touched, for people do not play gay, friendly jokes on those whom they do not like or trust.

Sue rarely came back to the office at noon, now, but lunched in the district, as she had done at Henry Street. She still missed the crowded colour and gaiety of the East Side, but the problems in Harlem were much the same. Could she persuade the widowed mother of two children to put them in a temporary home and go away for a rest? What was to be done about fifteen-year-old Minnie Battle, whose husband had deserted her? Would Jake Flue stop drinking and keep the job Sue had found for him? And *what* was she to do about John Kelly's baby?

John Kelly's baby was rapidly becoming a thorn in Sue's flesh. The Kellys were Scottish – a father and three children. There were two boys of nine and ten, and a baby girl, six months old. The mother had died two months before.

An unhappy but determined Mr Kelly had stopped Sue in the street and begged her to find a place for the baby – 'a real home, with nice folks – somewhere near here – so I can see her every day.'

'You mean you want her adopted?' Sue asked.

'Oh, no!' he said, shocked. 'I just want her to have a mother's care. I – I can pay three dollars a week for it.'

'I suppose you wouldn't consider putting her in a children's home?'

'No, ma'am, I wouldn't. I want her where I can have some say about her. I can't keep her home because I'm workin' all day, and at night it's all I can do to get the boys fed and clean and into bed. They're all right, because they're in school – but the baby needs a woman's care.'

'Where's the baby now?'

'She's in a day nursery – but that ain't no help at night.' He tugged at Sue's sleeve in desperation. 'Please, nurse – you get around everywhere – you could find somebody.'

'I'll try,' Sue promised, 'but it may take a long time.'

'Well, I hope it don't, because I'm 'most crazy. But if it does – I'd rather wait and get along's best I can than put her in an institution. You *will* look, nurse?'

Sue had tried, but so far had been unsuccessful, and Mr Kelly gave her no peace. Whenever she passed the bakery where he worked he dashed out to urge and plead, 'as if,' thought the harassed Sue, 'I could produce a home, like a rabbit, out of a hat.'

All this was distracting. In addition, August was extremely hot, and explosive with thunderstorms, so that between broiling in the sun, being drenched by violent showers, teaching the rudiments of health and sanitation, doing dressings, giving baths, pacifying Mr Kelly, and untangling other people's difficulties, Sue was on the verge of forgetting that she had a difficulty of her own.

It was forced upon her attention again, very unexpectedly, toward the end of the second week in August – only a few days before Connie's wedding and Bill's expected arrival in New York.

The day began like any other, with the usual morning visits, each of which seemed the most important until the next came along. After lunch Sue telephoned the office to ask if there were any new calls.

'There's one,' Miss Farrar's crisp voice announced. 'And you'd better go at once. It sounds like an emergency.'

'What is it?'

'I don't know – couldn't find out. Somebody called up and said they thought a woman named Adams, in the next house to theirs, was very sick. That's all I got.'

She gave Sue the address and hung up.

Sue pulled her hat down to shade her eyes from the glare of the street, picked up her bag, and set out for the address. She found it without difficulty – a dingy brownstone house in a dingy street that was as hot as a breath from a furnace. The house steps were dirty, and there was only a hole where the bell should have been.

She knocked several times and got no response, but at last she heard a shuffle of footsteps coming slowly and heavily towards the door. There was an instant of silence, and Sue felt that she was being looked at. Then the door opened.

Sue found herself looking into the tiny, bloodshot eyes of a bald man with a thick nose and an enormous paunch. He wore only an undershirt and trousers, the braces dangling, and his breath was raw with whisky.

'Whadda ya want?' he demanded.

'I'm the Henry Street nurse,' said Sue pleasantly, 'and I've come to see Mrs Adams.'

'Well, ya can't! This is a private residence – see! An' nobody wants ya here.'

'But,' said Sue patiently, 'someone does want me.

They telephoned for me. If you'll just let me come in –'

The man's huge bulk filled the doorway.

'How do I know who ya are? Ya got identification?'

Sue pointed to her uniform and bag. 'These are identification enough,' she said quietly. 'Let me come in, please.'

'I tell ya there ain't nobody sick here!'

'Suppose you let me decide that after I've seen Mrs Adams.'

'You get the hell away from here!'

'I'll do nothing of the sort.'

'Oh, ya won't, won't ya? We'll see about that! If you ain't down to the corner in one minute I'm gonna call the p'lice.'

Sue laughed amiably. 'Do,' she said. 'I'll wait.'

The man hesitated. Then, in a slightly milder tone, 'Now looka here, kid, I don't wanna be too hard on ya. Ya wouldn' like bein' in jail. If ya beat it without no fuss I won't say nothin' to the p'lice.'

'I'm sorry, but I couldn't possibly go until I've seen Mrs Adams.'

Okay, sister, ya ast for it!'

There was a telephone in the hall and he shuffled back to it, coughing importantly, and turning once to look back. Sue hadn't moved.

He picked up the receiver, growling in his throat, and dialled.

'Hello? Gimme the Sergeant! Hello? Sergeant? I gotta woman here – tryin' to break in – yessir – says she's a nurse!' He laughed hoarsely. 'Nossir – never seen her before. Yessir.' He turned to Sue. 'C'mere, you! He wants ta speak to ya – an' ya better be careful.'

Sue took the warm, greasy receiver, holding it gingerly away from her ear.

'Hello? Sergeant O'Day? This is Sue Barton.'

'Barton!' said the receiver violently. 'Well, I'll – What's the trouble, Miss Barton? Are ye all right? Want me to send a squad car around?'

'Oh, no, don't send anybody. I'm all right. But there's a sick woman in the house, and this man won't let me see her.'

'He won't, eh? Well, ye trot right along to yer patient. I'll fix that guy. Put him on again.'

Sue handed the man the telephone without a word, and saw the colour drain from his face as the receiver barked and snapped. She left him there, and went upstairs to the third floor and a dim, stifling room.

It was bare of furniture, except for a bed, on which lay a hollow-eyed woman who was barely conscious, and roused with difficulty. She stared up at Sue with glazing eyes.

'Who – are – you?' she whispered.

'I'm the nurse,' said Sue gently. 'How long have you been like this?'

'Three – days.'

Sue bit back a furious exclamation, and, finding no place except the floor for her bag, spread down paper napkins and set to work. The woman's temperature was 103, and her pulse was a faint, twitching thread, barely discernible.

'Who is your doctor, Mrs Adams?' Sue asked.

'I – haven't – any. He – wouldn't – let –'

'Why?' Sue demanded, and became aware of the silence downstairs.

'I – owe – two months' – rent. He – took my – furniture –'

'Have you had anything to eat to-day?'

The waxen face turned on the pillow. 'I couldn't –'

Sue bent over. 'Listen, Mrs Adams, I think it would be better if you were in a hospital. I'll make you a little more comfortable, and then I'll go and call an ambulance.'

'It's no – use.' Mrs Adams paused – struggled – went on. 'He won't – let – me – get away – until – I've – paid –'

'Oh, won't he! Just you relax while I give you a sponge, and leave everything to me.'

Deftly, Sue bathed the hot body. It lay much too still under her hands. When she had finished she said, 'I'm going downstairs for a minute. I'll be right back.'

Mrs Adams stirred and opened her eyes. 'Be – careful – he –'

'Don't you worry!'

Sue ran lightly down the stairs – but that was as far as she got; for at the bottom her way was barred. The man stood there breathing noisily, one hand on the banister, the other against the wall.

'I heard ya!' he said. 'You ain't takin' nobody outa this house without I say so – see? Thought ya'd get me in bad with the p'lice, didn't ya!' He moved up a step, swaying.

Sue was too angry to be frightened.

'Let me pass, please,' she said.

He leered at her soddenly. 'Ya goin' ta stay right where y' are, baby.' He grinned. 'Pretty little cat, ain't ya!' The mottled purple of his hand slid along the wall and caught her suddenly by the wrist. His whisky breath came nearer and nearer.

Sue tried to jerk free, but his grip tightened – and

he laughed. 'C'mere –' he began. Then, catching a change of expression in Sue's eyes, he turned his head.

The door to the street was still open, and coming up the steps in great bounds was Sergeant O'Day, his face crimson with rage. Two patrolmen were close on his heels. Beyond them, shining in the sun, was a green and white car.

It was all over very quickly with a snapped, 'Take him in, bhoys!' and an unsteady shuffling, out the door and down the steps. But when the Sergeant turned to Sue, she had gone – to the telephone – up the stairs – into the stifling room. It was not until the ambulance had carried away the still figure of Mrs Adams that Sue broke down.

She was no weeper, but her eyes filled when the Sergeant put a great, fatherly arm about her.

'There now – there now!' he said. 'Did ye think I wud heed yer foolish little orders to send nobody? Shure an' I cud hear the man was dhrunk over the telephone.'

Sue wiped her eyes with the back of her hand and laughed shakily. 'Golly!' she said, and looked up at the kindly face above the blue expanse of chest. 'You're – you're sweet, Sergeant O'day! Thank you *so* much!'

'Sweet, it is!' His laughter boomed. ''Tis a darter of Ireland ye should be, with yer red head an' yer blarneyin' ways.' He looked down at her tenderly. 'Arrah! 'Tis but a child ye are, an' I'm thinkin' that fine young feller will be thankin' me for this day.'

Sue nodded mistily.

'Live in New York, does he?'

'N–no – in New Hampshire. He's a doctor.'

'Away off there? Shure, an' the bhoy's crazy, lavin' ye here.'

Sue bent over to pick up her bag. Her voice came muffled. 'That's not his fault,' she said.

The Sergeant glanced at her sharply as she straightened up. 'Havin' a bit o' trouble, maybe?'

Sue nodded again.

'Ye won't mind an old man askin' – are yer for marryin' with him?'

'Yes, after – after a while.'

The broad, kind face sobered. 'Ye're here – an' he's there – an' ye'll marry him afther a while?' He put a gentle hand on her shoulder. 'Wud ye hark to a bit o' advice?'

'Gladly!'

'Well then – ye are a pretty lass and a fine one – as fine as ever a man cud ask – but don't ye forget – there's others as wud jump at the chancet to catch a nice young doctor – an' they're right on the ground, maybe.'

'Oh, but he isn't like that!' Sue cried, startled. 'Really, he isn't!'

The Sergeant shook his head. 'That's as is. But I'm tellin' ye – 'tis bad business – anny way ye look at it – to kape a man waitin' overlong.'

14
The Nineteenth of August

Grand Central Station, that late afternoon of August eighteenth, was a vast expanse of shining floors, soft lights, and great sweeping arc of ceiling, but Sue and Kit, waiting on the platform for the train from Chicago, were blind to decorative effects.

'We're terribly early,' Kit complained, standing on tiptoe to peer at the blackboard announcing the arrival of trains.

'Well –' Sue began in a judicial tone. It was her last attempt to be calm. She exploded an instant later. 'I'm so thrilled! I'm so thrilled to see Connie! I'm thrilled she's getting married! I'm thrilled the wedding's going to be in New York! I'm –'

'You're thrilled,' Kit said, grinning; and then, to no one in particular, 'It's probably a little trouble with her glands. Rest in a dark room, and five gallons of beef extract three times a day, would –'

'Nothing would,' said Sue firmly.

'Maybe you're right, at that. Sue – *why* isn't Connie's mother going to be at her wedding?'

'Officially because she's in Europe, and drinking mineral water or something. Actually, I think it's because Connie isn't marrying a title.'

'Well, it makes it nice for us, anyway. If she'd stayed away from Europe Connie would have been married at home, with a choir and cut-glass fruit dishes. This way, everything is just as Connie wants it – no fuss, and only us, and her father and Phil. And she can go right home with Phil, and not be pushed around any more.'

'Yes – which reminds me – where *are* the boys? I've never known anybody to be as vague as Bill about when they'd get here, or where they'd stay.'

'They'll probably –' Kit broke off suddenly as she caught sight of a tall young man hurrying towards them. He had dark hair and very clear, deep-set eyes. Kit's own eyes began to twinkle.

Sue, who had noticed nothing, was saying impatiently, 'Probably what?' when hands closed over her eyes and a familiar deep voice said cheerfully, 'Merry Christmas!'

Sue whirled round and found her nose pressed against a necktie. Her hat slid over one ear. Her gloves flew one way – her bag another. One of her bronze curls was entangled in a sleeve button.

'Bill!' she gasped, and stood motionless with shock. Then, laughing and a little tremulous, she untangled the curl. 'You – you idiot!' she said, recovering herself. 'Frankly, Dr Barry – aren't you a little old for this sort of thing?'

Bill's eyes were warm, resting on her upturned face. 'Much too old,' he said. 'Doddering.' He gathered up her scattered belongings. 'Carry your bag, miss? Fruit! Chocolate! Magazines! Chewing gum! Oh, *Sue* –' He kissed her swiftly and as swiftly stood back, to look at her again.

Sue thought with a pang, 'He's thinner and he looks tired.' Her smile at him was tender, but she said lightly, 'So nice, Dr Barry, meeting you in this informal way. And now, may I present my friend, Miss Van Dyke?'

'Lordy!' Bill turned to Kit, contrite. 'Kit, old thing! How are you! I'm so sorry! I'm afraid I –'

'Didn't see me!' Kit finished, openly laughing at him. 'Oh, well – in these cases of life and death one overlooks a lot. But Bill – what have you done with the bridegroom?'

'Gosh! I forgot him too! Behold!' He waved an arm towards the left.

The girls turned quickly and saw, standing a little apart from the crowd, a short, earnest young figure, whose grey eyes behind horn-rimmed glasses were fixed on the door. He was unaware of the girls, of Bill, of the station – all his consciousness drawn out to a single point, in a tensity of waiting.

'Phil!' the girls shrieked. 'Phil! Oh, *Mister* Saunders!'

He was blind and deaf.

They hurried across to him, Sue very much aware of Bill, close behind her. 'Phil! How are you? It's wonderful to see you –'

Phil turned unseeing eyes upon them. 'How do you do?' he said politely, lifting his hat.

Exasperated, Sue shook him by the arm. 'Phil Saunders – you stop that! Look – it's Sue Barton – remember me? I'll tell Connie if –'

'What?' said Phil, suddenly alert. 'Oh! Why, Sue – Kit! How – er –' His voice trailed away and his eyes returned to the platform.

'Better leave him alone,' Bill said. 'He'll come out of it after a while – I hope. But there's no use bothering him now.'

They waited impatiently, talking of this and that, with long silences between. Bill's coat sleeve was rough under Sue's hand. She glanced up at him from time to time.

He caught one of these upward glances and smiled at her in silent content.

'The train,' Kit remarked suddenly, 'is in!'

They hurried forward to stand watching the first thin trickle of passengers through the archway.

'Why is it,' Sue demanded with bitterness, 'that the people you're meeting are always the last ones –'

She was interrupted by an inarticulate sound from Phil, and a cry from Kit. '*There she is!*'

A tiny figure in olive-green detached itself from the crowd and ran forward, straight to Phil.

The others discreetly turned their attention to Mr Halliday, whose fine, gentle face had been a little wistful looking after that running figure.

Connie remembered where she was at last. Flushed and incoherent, she flung an arm around each of the girls.

'You darlings!' she bubbled. 'How is everything? Isn't this *gorgeous*? I thought the train would never stop – I mean come – and – oh, dear!'

'Just let it go,' Kit said, hugging her. 'We know just how you feel. Or anyway – we think we do! So don't worry.'

Two taxis were required to get them all away from Grand Central. Connie and Phil were bundled into one. Bill and the girls, with Mr Halliday, took the other. There would be no chance, to-day, Sue thought, for any talk with Bill – and perhaps it was just as well. They were both excited and not very sensible. After another day they'd be more themselves.

There was a hasty tea in the hotel suite.

'Where's your orphan of the storm?' Connie asked, during a pause. 'Your ghost – I mean Marianna.'

'Oh,' said Sue. 'She couldn't get off to come, and anyway, she was feeling shy about it.'

'But she's coming to dinner to-night, isn't she? Do bring her!'

'We'd love to. We – I took the liberty of asking her to the wedding – if you don't mind.'

'Sue!' cried Connie. 'I expected her! Don't be a lunatic. Oh girls, are we really together again? Am I really here?'

'You'd better be,' said Phil. 'I'm not going to marry a figment of the imagination.'

Sue caught a sudden intensity in Bill's eyes and flushed uncomfortably.

'Kit,' she said hastily, 'we'd better go on home and get dressed for dinner.'

'We'll come with you,' said Bill promptly, 'if I can pry Phil away. How about it, old man? Come on – you've got to change, too.'

Phil came, reluctantly. In the taxi going home, Kit said, 'Good heavens! Where are you boys staying? I never thought about it, in all the excitement.'

'We're staying quite near you,' said Bill. 'Right around the corner, in fact, at the Hotel Anchor.'

'Oh, no!' the girls cried, together. 'Bill, you *can't*!' And Sue added, 'It's an *awful* place!'

'What's the matter with it?' Bill asked lightly. 'It's quite near your house – and I thought we could come round for breakfast in the morning. Phil doesn't care where he stays. He won't even notice.'

'But Bill,' said Sue, 'have you seen it?'

'Why – er – yes, briefly. We found it in the telephone book and stopped to leave our bags. It seemed all right, and clean enough – and it's cheap.'

'It certainly is!' Kit put in. 'It's a transient hotel for sailors and third-rate travelling salesmen.'

Bill laughed, masculine and superior. 'Oh, that's all right. Men don't mind that sort of thing. We don't have to hobnob with any drunks, you know. And it's only for one night.'

'One night!' Sue cried. 'But I thought –'

'I'm terribly sorry,' Bill said miserably. 'I've *got* to take the midnight train back, to-morrow night. I'm the only doctor in Springdale, you know.'

'But *I* only have the morning off for the wedding. It never occurred to me you wouldn't be here over the week-end – and I'd have *all day*, Sunday.'

'Gosh!' Bill was stunned. 'You're only off in the morning? But that means that we'll only have to-morrow evening together, instead of all day.'

'I'm afraid so.'

They stared at each other with unhappy eyes, forgetting Phil and Kit, who wisely remained silent. The taxi rumbled on, homewards, and nothing more was said, either about time off or about the Hotel Anchor.

This last subject was revived, however, when the boys came to the little house to collect the girls for dinner. They were introduced to Marianna, resplendent in Kit's black taffeta evening dress, and it was Marianna who, after the introductions, spoke her mind about the Hotel Anchor.

'Gee – golly! You guys – I mean – you fellers – well,

heck! You can't stay in that joint. They ain't used to folks like you. You better get outa there!'

'But it's not so bad,' Phil said unexpectedly. 'It really is clean – and our room is all right.'

'Okay,' said Marianna. 'But don't say I didn't tell you,' she grinned. 'I'll bet they like to of died when they see – saw you in a monkey ja – evening clothes, with all them shirt fronts.'

Sue wondered what had come over Marianna, that she should be struggling with her English, but she understood after a moment, for Bill was smiling at Marianna – his most engaging smile, which had in it both warmth and a charming deference.

'They did seem a little faint,' he agreed.

It was all thanks to Bill, too, that the Halliday's hotel suite failed to reduce Marianna to a defiant confusion of double negatives and gutter slang. Whenever she seemed about to go off the deep end he engaged her in conversation. He was friendly and direct. He drew her out, and Connie, always discerning, aided and abetted him. Marianna bloomed. By the end of dinner she was taking her fair share of the conversation in a voice at least three tones lower than usual, and not a single 'Gee' escaped her.

'Good girl!' Sue whispered to her, as the party retired to the living-room for coffee.

Marianna grinned. 'It ain't so bad, once you get going,' she said. 'He's a swell feller – that Dr Barry. She added unexpectedly, 'He's crazy about you, ain't he? I been watchin' him.'

Sue held out her hand, on which, for the first time in public, she was wearing Bill's ring.

Marianna bent over it.

'Gee!' she said. 'Why, it's a *real* diamond, ain't it? He give it to you?'

Sue nodded.

'Golly!' said Marianna, awed. 'Then – then you're goin' to *marry* him?'

'I was planning on it,' said Sue, laughing.

'Yummy!' It was a cry straight from the heart.

Sue looked up, to find Bill's eyes on her, question-ing, intent, and she flushed. 'I wish he wouldn't keep looking at me like that,' she thought, and was relieved when, presently, a general stir indicated that the party was breaking up.

'Come on, children,' Kit said. 'If Connie is going to be married at eleven in the morning she ought to be getting some sleep – and so ought the rest of us.'

On the way home in the taxi Bill inquired briskly, 'What time is breakfast?'

'Seven-thirty,' said Marianna, who was getting it.

'We'll be there!' Bill said.

The boys didn't linger at the little house, for the girls were determined to go to bed at once.

Sue, however, lay awake for a long time, wide-eyed, arms under her head, staring at the ceiling and thinking about Bill. He had been quite as usual except for that questioning look – which gave her no real clue to what he was thinking. 'He's so darling,' she thought, 'and he can be so difficult. I do wish I knew which he was going to be.'

Marianna had said seven-thirty, and at seven-thirty on the dot the boys rang the front doorbell. Sue answered it.

'Good morning –' she began. 'Heavens! What *is* the matter. You look simply *awful*!'

'I guess you were right about the hotel,' Bill said sheepishly. 'But at that, you couldn't have known about Butch.'

'Butch?'

'Feed us, darling, and we'll tell you.'

Both of them were pale and hollow-eyed, and Bill's movements were stiff. He handed Kit the single orange blossom that Phil was to wear in his lapel. 'Put it in water, will you, please?' he said. 'Ouch!'

Phil grinned. 'I knew that last flop you took would get you in the shoulder.'

'Mercy!' Kit said. Then, to Phil, 'Whatever you two may have been up to, I must say you seem a little more conscious than Bill, and I thought bridegrooms were supposed to be –'

'All bridegrooms,' Phil said, 'don't have Butch around the night before, to distract them.'

'If you don't tell us this minute,' Sue cried, 'I'll burst! *Please* tell us!'

Over bacon and eggs and coffee the boys told their tale.

'He was a great big tough,' Bill said, 'and he lurched into our room about half-past one.'

'Why weren't you in bed?' Sue demanded.

'We were in bed. I was trying to persuade Phil that everything would be all right – and that I wouldn't forget the ring – that Connie wouldn't be late – that he really wasn't too hopelessly unworthy of her – when Butch seems to have heard us talking, and came in to be sociable.'

'Yes,' Phil said. 'He was very sociable. He came in singing – and he has quite a voice.'

'He stayed,' Bill put in, 'all night.'

'Yes – and you should have heard Bill singing "Swanee River" with him. Butch would have company. They sang it and sang it. Butch said he liked it – though it made him a little tearful.'

'Not so much as "Mother Machree,"' Bill said. 'He sobered over that – that was after he'd got into my dinner jacket. It didn't fit him.'

'But why didn't you throw him out, you goops?' Kit said.

'You haven't seen Butch.' This from Bill. 'Besides, when we suggested an early departure he cried bitterly and said if we put him out he'd sit outside the door and howl, because it was his night to howl.'

Phil chuckled suddenly. 'Bill had the time of his life. He and Butch played a lot of games, and they wrestled. They wrestled quite a lot – and Bill took an awful pounding. And then Butch sang again, for Bill to tap-dance.'

'I guess,' said Marianna, 'it was kind of a night.' She added with utter sincerity, 'Boy! I'd like to of been there!'

They were still laughing when the girls rose from the table.

'We've got to leave you, I'm afraid,' Kit said. 'Connie –'

Phil went white. 'I thought maybe I'd come along too,' he said, 'and see Connie for a minute.'

'Aw, *no!*' Marianna cried, horrified. 'It's bad luck for the groom to see the bride before she gets to the church. You guys stay right here, and come when it's time!'

Phil subsided.

'Now – now!' Kit soothed him. 'Everything is all

right. Bill will look after you, and get you there on time. Have you got the ring, Bill?'

'I have.'

'Good! And I think he ought to be there by a quarter to eleven.'

'At your service, madame,' said Bill, with a gingerly bow.

The two hours at the hotel were a confusion of Connie with flushed face and enormous eyes – of Mr Halliday, appearing and disappearing – of Marianna, excited and underfoot, while the girls dashed in and out of cupboards, hunted through bags and boxes, rustled in tissue paper, and mumbled through mouthfuls of pins.

Connie's dress was creamy-white, of heavy, beautifully cut crêpe-de-Chine, and the face veil on her tiny white hat gave a misty, unreal quality to her hazel eyes and the warm ivory of her skin. Phil's orange blossoms, gold, white, and green made the only definite accent of colour.

Marianna, very solid besides Connie's littleness, stared down at her, awed.

'Gee!' she said. 'I – I never thought anybody could be so – so elegant.'

The girls, now that everything was done, smiled uncertainly at this strange Connie, and an irrelevant, absurd picture flashed through Sue's mind of the night Connie and Kit had boosted her through the wrong window of the Nurses' Home.

She thought, with a pang of realization, 'We'll never be like that again!'

Mr Halliday seemed to have forgotten the girls and Marianna. He said, 'You're *sure*, Connie?' in a low voice.

'Very sure, Dad,' said Connie steadily.

The Little Church round the Corner has an air of kindliness and welcome. It is an old church, peaceful among its flowers and the greenness of small lawns. The city vibrates around it and does not disturb it. Tall buildings plunge the street beyond into blue shadow, but the little church basks in the sun. Its open door is an invitation to rest.

Silence fell on the party as they moved slowly along the path to the door. Connie's eyes were raised to her father's gentle face in something very like apology. Sue and Kit, their light dresses bright in the sun, followed behind with Marianna, who made the only remark.

'I never been in a church before,' she whispered.

The cool shadow of the door enveloped them and they heard the voice of the organ, beginning softly and swelling to a thunder of song.

Connie went steadily forward, her hand on her father's arm.

The bridal chapel is a tiny place of dim lights, stained-glass windows, and little square pews that smell of the woods. A sanctuary light, older than the church itself, hangs above the white and gold altar – which was banked now with flowers.

Two dark-clad figures waited there before the minister, whose prayer book lay open in his hand.

Phil's face was colourless and he stood as one carved from stone, his eyes on Connie, coming slowly up the aisle beside her father.

The voice of the organ died away. There was a little rustle of movement.

Sue, taking her place at Connie's left, as maid of

honour, met Bill's eyes and saw again that intent, questioning look. Then the minister began in a clear, firm voice the lovely old words of the marriage service.

'Dearly beloved, we are gathered together in the sight of God and the face of this company –'

Sue's pulse quickened. There would be a day when she would stand like this with Bill – when those words would be meant for her – 'to live together after God's ordinance in the holy state of matrimony . . . forsaking all others . . . as long as ye both shall live?'

Phil's voice rang through the chapel. '*I will!*'

Connie's responses were faint but clear. Phil began, 'I, Philip, take thee, Constance –'

Connie stirred, and her eyes went to Phil's face to remain there in a look of such utter surrender that Sue's throat ached. She glanced at Mr Halliday, whose moustache quivered uncontrollably for an instant. Then his face relaxed in sudden happiness.

At the end of the responses, while Phil still held Connie's hand, with the shining new ring upon it, the minister, instead of beginning the Lord's Prayer as was customary, paused and glanced at Connie. Then, into the stillness, dropping one by one in tender beauty, came these words:

'Entreat me not to leave thee, or to return from following after thee: for whither thou goest, I will go; and where thou lodgest, I will lodge: thy people shall be my people, and thy God my God: where thou diest, will I die, and there will I be buried: the Lord do so to me, and more also, if aught but death part thee and me.'

The voice ceased and Sue, openly in tears, heard a

faint sob behind her, though whether from Kit or Marianna she did not know.

The prayer followed, and the benediction. Then, at last, the words, 'I pronounce you man and wife.'

Connie lifted her face to Phil for his kiss, and the organ thundered again, filling the little chapel and overflowing into dim reaches beyond in great waves of sound. Connie, on her husband's arm, went back along the aisle with light steps. Outside, in the sudden release from tension, everybody talked at once, everybody laughed – a little hysterically. Their voices babbled: 'Why do people always cry at weddings?' . . . 'Connie, dear, that passage from Ruth was *lovely* – how did you ever happen to –' 'Well, Mrs Saunders –' 'Father dear –' 'Kit, was that you bellowing –'

Connie and Phil were leaving on an early afternoon train, and there would only be time for a hurried luncheon. The wedding party, still laughing and excited, was borne away to the hotel.

No one was aware of food, though everyone except the bride and groom ate heartily. Connie was toasted. There were brief, awkward speeches – and then it was all over.

Sue had kissed Connie good-bye as cheerfully as she could and was turning to look for Kit when she felt Bill's hand on her arm.

'How about one whole, extravagant minute to ourselves?' he said.

Sue followed him into the now deserted dining-room of the hotel suite, where Bill drew two chairs over to the window. They sat down, and there was a little pause. Bill's glance wandered over Sue's hair, over her delicate features. Then he said, smiling a little:

'I don't want to be stand-and-deliverish, but I guess my resistance is low. I – I couldn't help thinking it would be very pleasant to see you as the blushing bride, and I –' He paused and bent forward abruptly. 'How much longer must I wait, Sue?'

Distressed, Sue hesitated. 'But Bill,' she said at last, 'we agreed that I was to have a little time for myself, first.'

'I know we did – but hasn't all this done anything to you at all?'

'Of course it has, Bill dear. Don't be an idiot! I was all sloppy, and I almost popped out with the responses myself.'

'*Did* you? Then – oh, Sue, why not? I mean, say, next month? There isn't any real reason, is there, why we shouldn't?'

Kit's voice in the entry said, '*Here* they are, Marianna!' She descended on them. 'Come on, you two! Bill, Sue has to be on duty in an hour!'

Bill rose at once.

'I'll call for you at seven-thirty,' he said to Sue.

'Why so formal?' Kit said, laughing. 'She gets home at half-past five.'

'Come at six, Bill.' Sue's eyes were pleading.

'All right,' he said.

Sue hurried out after Kit, desperately thankful for a little more time.

15
A Quiet Afternoon

It was unfortunate for everyone – except Sue's patients – that her afternoon turned out as it did. When Sue left – in fact, fled from – Bill, at the hotel, she was expecting to make a few visits to chronics, with perhaps one or two extra calls. August is not a busy month at Henry Street, and with an easy afternoon's work she could prepare for the struggle with Bill. She would have to be very tactful, for he was in anything but a reasonable frame of mind.

'There's no use in my being so upset and panicky,' she warned herself, as she changed into uniform at the office. 'I've known all along that this was coming, and all I can do is my best. If I have a quietish afternoon I can get myself together, and then we'll see.'

The familiar blue dress was cool on her shoulders and comforting; everything pertaining to it was so sure. She picked up her bag, grinned at Miss Farrar, and, collecting all her call slips, departed. There was only one new case, and it wasn't an emergency. Sue breathed a sigh of relief, happily unaware that the few minutes required to take her out of the building and into her district would be her last dull minutes that day.

Things began to happen at once, and they continued to happen with a kind of frantic perversity, as if, Sue thought afterwards, they knew about Bill, and were happening *at* him. In all her months at Henry Street Sue had never had such a day as this became, nor did she ever have another quite like it.

On the first street corner in her district she was greeted by an excited child. 'Come quick, nurse! Baby's fell out the window. Mamma tripped an' spilled him!'

The baby was not seriously injured, but Sue had the frightened mother to calm, and the ambulance to call. The baby's father couldn't be located. The grandmother had an attack of asthma, brought on by the excitement.

All through it the baby's aunt, a pitifully malformed hunchback, was Sue's right hand. She was deft with the baby, firm with its mother. And she carried out orders with an extraordinary self-confidence. Sue was amazed. Here was no embittered helpless cripple, but a self-reliant young woman whose deformity might exist in the minds of others, but never in her own.

The grandmother, between wheezes, explained it.

'She had a spinal sickness when she was a baby – it made her like that. I like to have lost my mind – thinking of her growing up to be like that – helpless. The doctors said nothing could be done for her. But Miss Wald thought different.'

'*Miss Wald!*'

The old woman smiled, remembering back across the years. 'We lived on the East Side, then, and Miss Wald, she heard about Millie. She always knew about folks in trouble. So she came, and she kept my courage up. It was her arranged for Millie to go to a school for crippled children, so she could grow up to

look out for herself. It was her said we should treat
Millie as if nothing was the matter with her. Millie
earns a real good living now. She's smart with her
hands – and she makes things and sells 'em through
the school. She – she's been just like anybody all her
life.'

Sue looked with awed eyes at the little hunchback
who had actually been Miss Wald's patient! Miss
Wald 'always knew about folks in trouble.' She
would, of course. 'And we're carrying on for her,
still,' Sue thought. '*I'm* carrying on for her! Oh, Bill –
why can't you see!'

Sue left the apartment at last, and set out to visit her
chronic invalids.

A few yards down the street she noticed a three-
year-old child wavering along the sidewalk, one small
hand covering his eyes from the light – although the
street was in complete shadow.

Sue looked at him sharply and then bent down.

'Hello, sonny! What's your name?'

The boy squinted at her. 'Jimmy,' he said.

'Jimmy what?'

He didn't know.

'Well, Jimmy, would you let me look at your eyes a
minute?'

He nodded, docile, like most children.

Sue tipped his little face up and peered into the
great black eyes. They had a strange, milky cloudness
in their depths.

Sue's heart sank. 'Cataract!' she thought. 'And in
both eyes.'

'Where do you live, Jimmy?' she asked gently.

He pointed vaguely back along the street towards a

group of young black women talking and laughing on a doorstep. Sue took him by the hand and approached the group.

'Which of you is Jimmy's mother?'

Someone said, 'Why, she was right here a minute ago, ma'am. I dunno where she went.'

Sue tried the house. The caretaker said Mrs Johnson came in just now, but went out again – maybe she went to the shop. The shopkeeper was amiable. Yes, she'd been here, but she was gone now. Try the chemist's. The chemist had noticed her passing – she went up that way.

The woman was discovered at last – across the street from the spot where Sue had found Jimmy. She was an intelligent and educated young woman who required no detailed explanation.

'He – he isn't going to be *blind*, is he?' she gasped, her eyes pleading for reassurance.

'Not if you get him to your doctor at once.'

The woman swallowed. 'Th-thank you, nurse – so much! I never dreamed – I – we thought – his clumsiness was because he's a baby. We thought he'd outgrow it. If – if I'd known –'

'Don't worry,' Sue assured her. 'We've found it in time. I'm sure he'll be all right.'

'I'll never forgive myself! If it hadn't been for your noticing –'

Sue continued on her way, hurrying now. She'd have to skip some of her regular calls if she was to see the new case – and she must. 'If it hadn't been for your noticing –' That was just it; she'd been trained to notice. Henry Street had trained her – Henry Street, which felt a responsibility for every human being in trouble, and never shirked that responsibility. 'And yet,' Sue thought bitterly, 'Bill thinks I ought to walk out on mine!'

Her next case was a dressing, which she did in record time, and hurried on. She never reached her chronic arthritis patient, however, for her way led her down a deserted side street and past a lorry that was drawn up beside the kerb.

A frightened masculine voice came from behind the lorry. 'My God, Mike! It don't stop! Here – try this!' A large, grimy hand reached down, pawed in the gutter, and came up with a dirty piece of newspaper.

Curiosity – or instinct – led Sue over to the kerb behind the lorry.

Two white-faced lorry drivers stood there. One of them was dabbing frantically – with the dirty newspaper – at great spurts of blood which shot from his wrist. The other man looked on, helpless.

Neither was aware of Sue until she sprang between them, her slim fingers closing on the wrist below the wound. The blood stopped spurting – and poured, instead. Sue jerked his arm up as high as she could reach.

'There's a piece of rubber tubing in my bag!' she said to the other man. 'Get it out! Hurry!'

He hurried, fumbling with unfamiliar straps until Sue could have screamed.

She snatched the tubing out of his hand. There was no time to be polite with a man bleeding to death before her eyes. The tubing coiled around his arm – slipped – caught! She tightened it with all her strength, and gave a gasp of relief as the pulsing blood slowed to a trickle, dripped for a moment, and then – stopped.

Her patient's face was like parchment and he was trembling with weakness.

'Here – sit down!' she urged, and he dropped to the kerb. Sue turned to the other man. 'What happened?'

'We was unloadin' soda-water bottles, an' one exploded – just before you came along.'

'Well – don't ever stuff a cut with dirty newspapers. It isn't healthy!'

She must clean the wound before infection started. Thank heaven for the faithful bottle of green soap solution. But she must have water for it, and the man was in no condition to be kept waiting. Soda water? It was as good as any.

Sue pulled a bottle out of a case and knocked the cap off. Then, while the half-flinching lorry driver leaned against her and a little knot of people gathered to watch, she cleansed the jagged wound with soda water and green soap, bandaged it with strips torn from her apron case, for she had used her last roll of bandage fifteen minutes before – and fastened the whole with a piece of tape for extra pressure.

'There!' she said. 'No – don't stop for thanks. I'll take it for granted. Get him onto that lorry and off to the hospital as quickly as you can!'

Together they bundled the patient into the seat and the lorry plunged away.

She wiped her face with a paper napkin. 'Whew!' she said aloud. 'What a quiet afternoon!' And it *would* be to-day that everything was happening. She grinned suddenly. 'All I need,' she thought, 'is a galloping horse and a couple of yips – and it's hurrah boys! Henry Street to the rescue!'

She washed her hands with the rest of the soda water, packed up her bag, and went on. There would be no time now for the chronics. They were mostly drop-in visits, anyway, and would be all right. She'd better get on to the new case. Sue looked at the call slip. The patient was a Mrs Yoland, and the address was not in the black section, but at one of the better apartment houses in the white district.

Mr Yoland opened the front door for Sue. He had come home from his store purposely to meet the Henry Street nurse. Mrs Yoland was nowhere to be seen.

The history of the case was clear-cut – and pathetic.

Nine years ago, the man told Sue, they had lost their baby. They had never had another. 'Seems like she's brooded and brooded about it,' he said. 'She cried for most two years, and then, after that, she got so she wouldn't go out – said the crowds scared her. She hasn't been outside the house in three years.'

'She keeps up with her housework,' Sue remarked, looking around the pleasant, orderly living-room.

'Yes, she does – always did. But she's so quick about it she gets done in two hours – and then she just sits and looks at the goldfish. She – she looks at 'em all day.'

'I should think the Mental Hygiene Clinic could help her.'

'Yes, miss. That's what I thought, but the doctor says there's no need.'

'Who is your doctor?'

He gave her the name of a man strongly suspected by the nurses to be a fake. The Department of Health had been watching him, but so far had been unable to produce any real evidence against him. Consequently, Sue's hands were tied. She couldn't take the woman to any clinic, since the doctor disapproved. There was nothing she could do, except apply a little mental hygiene herself, in the home.

'Suppose I talk to her, now,' she said.

'Certainly, Miss – Miss Barton, is it? If you'll excuse me – it takes a little time to persuade her to see anyone.' He turned back in the doorway. 'If you can think of *anything* that will help her – I'll back you, no matter what it is!'

While Sue waited in the sunny living-room she, too, watched the goldfish, and thought hard and earnestly, trying to put herself in this woman's place – trying to feel the bleak despair – the agony that had culminated in a kind of mental suicide. She was afraid, her husband said. She was afraid of people; afraid of crowds; afraid to go out. And she wanted a baby. If life wouldn't give her one she would have nothing to do with living.

A baby was all she needed, really, Sue was positive.

'But I can't just create a baby out of thin air,' Sue thought. 'I wonder – oh!' She was on her feet, flushed with the excitement of a new and splendid idea – if it would work. She sobered. Perhaps it wouldn't. She had better be careful.

There was a timid step in the doorway. Sue turned and saw a slim, brown-haired woman who wiped constantly at trembling lips with a crumpled handkerchief.

Sue felt herself to be seven feet tall and ominous, and she sat down quickly. This was not the moment for etiquette.

'I hope you don't mind my dropping in, Mrs Yoland,' she said quietly, and smiled her warm young smile.

Mrs Yoland's eyes flickered. 'How do you do,' she said faintly.

'It's so warm out,' Sue went on. 'I wonder if I might have a drink of water?' This was a long chance. Either the familiar activity would take Mrs Yoland's attention from her fear – or it would give her a chance to vanish into the back of the house and not return. Sue made her expression as appealing and fragile as she could.

The slim figure turned without a word and disappeared, to return a moment later with a glass of water. Sue drank slowly. 'What lovely goldfish,' she said. 'You know, I've never had any goldfish. Are they hard to take care of?'

'No.' Mrs Yoland hesitated. Then she said, 'They're very little trouble really.'

Sue developed a passionate interest in goldfish, asking more questions about them than she would have believed it possible for anyone to ask. But it had the desired effect; for once she was launced on this favourite topic Mrs Yoland's nervous terrors eased away, and she talked quite freely – even, after a while, sitting beside Sue on the couch.

Sue had no time to prepare any method of approach, but Mrs Yoland didn't seem as bad as she had expected – for people who are seriously disturbed mentally do not respond as readily as Mrs Yoland was doing, or follow leads as quickly. The leads had been carefully chosen, it was true – but she *did* respond. 'The whole thing,' Sue decided, 'is a lot more superficial than it seems. I'll bet the way to do is to be quite simple and direct – now she's found she can talk to me.'

And so, after a little, Sue remarked casually, 'I suppose you're wondering why I came, Mrs Yoland. Your husband asked me to come, and now I'm here I've a suggestion I want to make.'

There was a guarded look in Mrs Yoland's eyes, but she said nothing – waiting.

Sue went on. 'There's a man in my district whose wife has just died, leaving him with three children. One of them is a baby girl, six months old.'

'Oh!' Mrs Yoland cried. 'The poor little thing!'

'It is rather pitiful, isn't it? Mr Kelly is a good man, and a splendid father, and it's breaking his heart to have to put the baby in an institution. He wants her to have a good home, and a mother's care – wants to board her somewhere permanently.'

Mrs Yoland was listening now, eagerly.

'I – I thought,' Sue went on, 'that perhaps you'd be interested. The baby is a lovely little thing – all round and roly-poly, with dimples in her knees. But she won't be like that much longer if she's neglected – and he can't take care of her, Mrs Yoland. Wouldn't you like to have her?'

The corners of Mrs Yoland's mouth had curled upward in a smile when Sue spoke of the baby's dimpled knees. Now she sprang to her feet in tremulous excitement.

'*Could* I have her? Would he let me?'

'Well, he asked me to find just the right home for her, and I think this is it. He said he'd trust me.'

'W-*when* could I have her? Could I have her *now* – to-day?'

Sue laughed. 'I think probably. Of course, I'll have to see him first. But he's so anxious for her to be taken care of. You understand, he isn't giving up his paternal interest in her. He will pay for her care. And he wants to see her often.'

'Of course! I understand. Oh, Miss Barton – *please* bring her to-day!'

'But have you got things for her?'

'Oh, I can borrow some, just until I can go out and buy my own. I've a neighbour across the street – her children are big now. She has a cot, and a little bath-tub, and –'

'Where – were you planning to shop for her?'

'Oh,' said Mrs Yoland absently, 'I'll just run down to-morrow and look round the department stores.'

Sue could have shouted.

There was an odd sound in the doorway and she looked up. How long had Mr Yoland been standing there? He was motionless, his face utterly without expression, and Sue wondered if he knew that tears were streaming down his face.

She rose hastily. 'You can borrow the cot, Mrs Yoland – and I'll go right now and see the baby's father. I think I can promise to bring the baby back with me.'

'Oh – Miss Barton! Do you think she'll like me? I – I know I'm not going to sleep a wink all night – I'm so excited.'

Sue laughed and hurried away – almost running the whole way to the bakery in spite of the heat. She burst in without ceremony.

'John!' she cried. 'Oh, John – *I've got a home for the baby*!'

'Glory be, Miss Barton!'

'Could you leave – to get her ready to-day?'

'I can't – but I will. It'll be a load of worry off me, and the quicker the better for the baby.'

'Oh, John! I'm so glad. They want her terribly! They *need* her! I'll tell you about it on the way. You'll come to the house with me, won't you?'

'You bet I'll come, Miss Barton!'

John came, trundling the crowing baby in a shabby pram. He had packed her clothing with the utmost care. He brought her toys – her hairbrush – a little locket which had been his wife's.

And from the window Mrs Yoland watched the little procession – as long as she could stand it. Then she vanished, to reappear on the steps.

Sue dropped back a little. She wouldn't interfere with this meeting for the world. Mr Yoland, apparently, had the same idea, for Sue caught a glimpse of him in the hall watching his wife with an anxious, tender smile.

John came on, stout and clumsily male, holding bundles at awkward angles and pushing the baby's pram without regard for unevenness on the path. A teddy bear bulged under his arm. A toy monkey on a stick thrust upwards close to his ear. A paper bag full of blocks leaned against his chest.

Mrs Yoland came down the steps, very slowly, her eyes fixed on the bouncing baby. She seemed ten years younger. The pram had almost reached the steps when Mrs Yoland raised her eyes and looked at the stumbling awkward John – over his child's bobbing head. John returned the look in silence.

'I'm pleased to meet the baby's mother,' John said gravely.

'And *I'm* pleased to meet the baby's father. Will you come in?'

'Don't mind if I do.'

Mrs Yoland bent over and lifted the baby from the pram. John picked up the bundles, and then, side by side, they went up the steps and into the house. Mr Yoland beckoned to Sue, but she shook her head. 'To-morrow!' she called.

She glanced at her watch. It was a quarter past seven – and Bill was coming for her at six.

16
Whose Fault?

The roof garden was very smart, and very expensive –
a suaveness of silver-grey and black, with casual
thrusts of terra cotta, all mirrored in the polished
green floor. Amber lights were soft on the tables, on
gleaming shirt fronts and bare shoulders. Delicate
china quivered to the low beat of music, and beyond
the parapet, far below, Manhattan was black silk,
pricked and striped with gold.

Sue and Bill had a table near the dance floor, but
they were not dancing, and they had not been eating
very much. They agreed that it was too hot to eat –
though the roof was so cool that Sue was still wearing
a brief jacket over the jade-green chiffon of her
evening gown. She was playing absently with a spoon
while she stared at the dancers, her red hair a flame
against silver and black.

Bill was lounging in his chair, hands deep in his
trousers pockets, gazing at his own silk-clad ankle.
The amber lighting had erased the shadows under his
eyes and he looked younger – but very wistful.

Sue glanced at him. Poor darling – he had been so
nice about that hour-and-a-half wait, saying pleasantly that it didn't matter. There had been no time, at
the house, for detailed explanations, and in the taxi
going he had talked about Springdale. It was in the
heart of the White Mountains, he said – as though Sue

had not been born in New Hampshire. It was a wild, rugged country, incredibly beautiful. Now, in summer, the little villages were green and white among the foothills, and great cloud shadows drifted across blue peaks. In autumn the air was as cold as spring water and white mists curled in the valleys. And if she could only see a blizzard get up and dance on the face of a mountain – or long lines of snow wavering across the open fields, burying the stone walls, and making white triangles of spruce and hemlock!

The contrite Sue didn't remind him that she was as familiar with her native state as it was possible to be, and asked tactfully eager questions about Springdale.

Bill seemed to have forgotten that he had told her all about it long since, and explained that Springdale's population was only two hundred, but that the outlying farms and other small villages raised the number of his potential patients to nearly eight thousand. Once or twice he took a quick breath and seemed on the point of telling her something special – but each time he broke off. And he had not so much as touched her hand all evening.

Now, with dinner almost over, the conversation was dying an unnatural death. Sue had tried to revive it, and failed miserably. At last she said, 'Bill dear–?'

Bill stared a moment longer at his ankle. Then he looked up, squaring his shoulders.

'I suppose we might as well come to it,' he said. 'Is there some real reason why we shouldn't be married next month?'

'I'm afraid there is,' said Sue miserably. 'You see, we ought to stay on a reasonable length of time after we've had our training. They pay us while we're being trained, so that they're really out of pocket on us. It wouldn't be fair of me to leave before I've made some return.' She hesitated, playing nervously with the spoon. Then, 'Henry Street isn't like other organizations, Bill. I – I just can't go up to them after six months of training, and say brightly, "Well, thanks for the buggy ride – I'll be toddling along."'

Bill grinned faintly. 'Well,' he said, 'as Butch remarked last night– "I don't get youse." What's different about this buggy ride?'

'It's the kind you don't walk home from in the middle of. Listen – this afternoon –' She told him the story of the afternoon, in detail. Bill listened, interested, but when she had finished he said:

'Of course, darling, everybody knows that Henry Street does a great deal of good, and while I hate to reveal my dumbness in all its glory – I have to admit that I don't get the point of all this.'

Sue flushed. He was making it very hard. 'I'd hoped,' she said, 'that you'd see the point as I went along.'

'Sorry. What is the point?'

'The point,' said Sue slowly, 'is that this afternoon was typical of the work of an organization which functions, not for gain, but solely for the benefit of other people. It isn't grabbing anything except a chance to make things better when they're worse – if you follow me. Its whole policy is based on kindness and understanding and justice.'

'Well?'

'Well, I don't want to seem dreary, but there isn't very much of that kind of thing in the world, and I think Henry Street deserves something better than to have its nurses run out on it the moment they have enough training to be useful.'

Bill considered this in silence. Then he said, 'How many nurses at Henry Street?'

'I don't remember the exact number – between two and three hundred. There's always a waiting list.'

'In other words, New York's poor are having everything possible done for them.'

'Why yes, I should hope so, but –'

Bill straightened in his chair and leaned forward.

'Listen, sweet – in Springdale the nearest hospital is fifty miles away – over mountain roads. There are no nurses nearer than that, and I'm the only doctor. They have no one else to help them when they're sick, or when there are accidents. You can do the same kind of thing there that you're doing here – and the need is far greater. We can work *together* – and really build up something. It'll be hard – we'll have to get up in the night and plough through storms, and ford rivers – maybe leave our car and hoof it for miles – to deliver a baby – or to stop a haemorrhage – or fight pneumonia or snake-bite in some lonely farmhouse. There'll be gunshot wounds and concussions, and fractures, and influenza. There'll be emotional crises and domestic tragedies. There have even been murders – which could have been prevented by a little mental hygiene. Those people need you more than you're needed here – where there are hordes of doctors and nurses and clinics.'

Sue's eyes were shining. She had forgotten the issue at stake, seeing only the lonely little villages and their need. She knew those sturdy people – knew their limitations and their depths, their kindness and their obstinacy – knew their hard struggle for existence.

'Oh, Bill!' she cried. 'I'll be *crazy* about it!'

Bill shot up in his chair, his face glowing.

'*Then you'll do it?*'

The eager light vanished from Sue's eyes. 'Darling, I *can't*! Don't you see? I'll come as soon as I can – and we'll have all the rest of our lives together. But I *have* to do this first.'

Bill's face darkened. 'I think,' he said quietly, 'that you're being a lot too idealistic to make sense. You're going around in a kind of rosy glow of nobility and self-sacrifice.' He sat for a moment, thinking. Then he said, 'Have you said anything to them about leaving?'

'Why, no, of course not.'

'Then you don't know what they'd think about it! Have you got a contract with them?'

'No – none of the nurses have.'

'For heaven's sake, Sue! What is all this? Do they say, definitely, that they expect you to stay on?'

'N-no. But they do say that a nurse isn't really useful until she's been on a district for at least a year and –'

'Do you mean to sit there and tell me that that's all you've got to go on? You haven't any contract – nobody has said you have to stay any particular length of time – you say yourself that you've never asked them a thing about it – and that they have a waiting list of nurses!'

'But Bill, dear – it isn't so much what they might think about it as how I *feel* about it. I can't seem to make you understand.'

'I think I do understand – very well. Suppose you

were sick? Henry Street would go on without a hitch, wouldn't it?'

'Why yes – but if I were sick it wouldn't be my fault. If I was to walk out on them at this point it *would* be my fault – and I think it would be a rotten thing to do. When I came you said I was to have as much time as I liked. I had no way of knowing that you'd change your mind. I thought you meant what you said.'

The waiter appeared, bearing coffee. When he had gone Bill said gloomily: 'That's perfectly true. But I think circumstances have always altered cases – and I think my not having the slightest idea how – how dambably hard – this wait would be – alters everything.'

Sue made no reply. Her face was a little pale now.

'Did it ever occur to you,' Bill went on, 'that since you did promise to marry me you ought to consider my wishes? Men are supposed to have *some* say about what their wives do. I'm asking you again – for the last time – will you marry me next month?'

Sue, dazed by this tone, didn't see the desperation in his eyes. 'I – I can't, Bill. *Please* try to understand. And it – it isn't so much longer, really. A – a year and a half – more – because that would make it two years altogether, and –'

'*A year and a half more!*' Bill sat back and looked out across the plain of tables, his young face set and stern. Sue rested her chin in an unsteady hand and watched him, distressed. He turned his head at last, slowly, and looked at her.

'You don't really love me enough, do you?' he said.

Sue gasped. 'Bill! How can you –'

'I can, because it seems pretty evident that if you

loved me I'd be more important to you than this vague idealism about Henry Street.'

Sue's lips were a white line. 'You don't really love me, either, or you'd have some respect for the way I feel and for what's important to me. You couldn't ask me to do something I feel isn't fair.'

'You wouldn't feel one way or another about it – if you loved me. Nothing else would matter.'

'That works two ways – doesn't it?' There were bright spots of colour on Sue's cheeks. Her eyes, meeting Bills, were hotly accusing. 'You're only thinking about yourself. You don't care what you do to me, as long as you get your own way!'

Bill shifted his position to face her squarely. 'Did you ever hear,' he said in a low voice, 'of the old saying about people who live in glass houses?'

They stared at each other, furious and horrified. They *couldn't* be saying these things to one another, flinging hard little words, like stones, in anger and bitterness. It wasn't real! It couldn't happen! All around them there was laughter, and the beat of music. In a moment they would laugh too, and get up and dance.

The moment passed in a silence as remote and frozen as the arctic seas.

Bill said, slowly, as before, 'So you're one of the career girls – who keep men dangling half their lives. I should have seen it!'

'And *I* should have believed you when you said you were old-fashioned – the kind of man who must *own* his wife – and rule her – as if she were half-witted!'

Bill's lips curled. 'It's lucky we found out in time, isn't it?' he said deliberately.

Sue looked at him for a long moment. Then her eyes cleared with sudden purpose.

'I take it from that,' she said, 'that you have no wish to plunge yourself into an unhappy marriage.' She paused. 'Well, neither have I.' Carefully, controlling the trembling of her fingers, she slipped off the diamond ring, dropped it on the table beside Bill's untouched coffee cup, and rose to her feet.

Bill stood up quickly, his face blank with shock.

Sue –' He picked up the ring uncertainly.

'I'm sorry it has to end like this, Bill.' Sue's voice had a thin, breathless quality, as if it came from far away. 'I – I wish you every happiness.' Then, as Bill remained staring at her, she turned blindly, and fled.

Bill stood where she left him until her curly red head had vanished from his sight. Then he lifted his hand with the movement of one asleep, and looked down at it. The diamond flashed on his palm, blue white – crystal and flame. He turned it over, staring at it, and turned it again.

It sparkled in his fingers, turning over and over in the amber light.

17

Marianna Lends a Hand

All the way home in the taxi Sue was stoney-eyed –
numb with shock. At the door of the little house she
paid the driver, went up the steps, and let herself in
quietly, so as not to disturb Marianna, sleeping on the
living-room couch.

Upstairs she undressed slowly and got into bed to
lie motionless, her arms limp at her sides. She lay for a
long time in this tightening coil of misery, not moving
– not even thinking.

Then, far away, above the murmur of the city, *a
train whistled*!

Sue lifted one hand in a blind gesture of protest and
something hot and wet trickled down her cheek. She
turned over suddenly, on her face. Her hands
clenched on the corners of the pillow and her body
shook. Sue, who never cried, was crying now – with
great wrenching sobs which hurt her chest, tore at her
throat, choking her. She tried to muffle them in the
pillow.

'*Bill!*' she whispered, '*Oh Bill – dear!*'

Sometime later her bedroom door opened. Sue
didn't hear it. A voice said, 'Gee, Sue! What's the
matter!'

Sue held back a sob desperately.

Marianna sat down on the bed and put an awkward
arm around the shuddering body. 'I heard you come

in,' she said, trying to speak casually. 'You – come home awful early, didn't you? I warn't asleep. Where was the boy-friend?'

'G-gone!'

'Shucks! You don't wanter take it like that. He hadda go – but he'll be back.'

Sue made no reply. She couldn't speak.

Marianna bent over her. 'Aw, now! Gosh!' She gathered Sue into her arms and held her, waiting for the storm to pass.

The sobs were beyond control and it was a long wait, but they spent themselves at last. Marianna remained silent, stroking the red head buried in her lap. Sue stirred presently and sat up.

'I'm all right now,' she said thickly.

'Wh-what was it, Sue? It ain't just because he hadda leave?'

For answer Sue held out her left hand. The red glow from the electric sign fell upon it.

'Your *ring*!' Marianna cried. 'You lost it off!'

'I gave it – back.' Sue's voice shook.

'*You gave it back!*'

Sue nodded. 'Could I – have a handkerchief – please?'

Marianna hunted through the chest of drawers and returned with the handkerchief. 'Here! Blow!'

Sue reached up for the handkerchief, her lips quivering like a hurt child's. 'Th-thanks,' she said. '*Oh Marianna!*' Her eyes filled again.

'What is it, kid? Can't you tell a feller?'

'There – isn't much to tell.' Her breathing was still difficult and she spoke with an effort. 'We – disagreed – about my work. I – we got mad – and said awful things.'

'But why?'

'Because he – wanted me to leave my job – and get married to him.'

'Aw!' Marianna was staggered. 'You mean to tell me that grand guy wanted to get married right off, an' you wouldn't?' She paused. 'Well,' she said, 'I guess you musta had a reason – but it ain't good enough.'

'That's what – he – said.' The whole story came out then, and Sue explained as best she could, trying to make clear her own attitude – and Bill's. 'He seemed to think,' she concluded, 'that our being engaged gave him the right to dictate to me. He – made my point of view seem awfully silly – and it's important to me. He ought to have respected that – and he didn't. Do you see?'

Marianna nodded. 'Sure I see – that you was both mad. He ain't like that underneath. He's a swell guy, an' he ain't the kind not to have respect for how other folks feel about things. If he wasn't he wouldn't have laid himself out to make a mutt like me feel important an' special. He's a prince! If he acted up it musta been because you got his goat.'

'Well – he got mine.'

'Gee, I'm sorry!' Marianna sat thinking. Then she said, 'Suppose it was to turn out that you was mistaken about it bein' lousy of you to leave Henry Street right off the bat? Seems like you kinder took it for granted. You might be wrong.'

Sue stared at her. 'But I wasn't, Marianna. Don't be silly!'

'You could ask 'em, at your office. 'Twouldn't do no harm, would it?'!

'Why no, only I don't see the necessity for it.'

'But suppose you *was* wrong?' Marianna persisted.

Sue shook her head. 'You don't understand, Marianna. I wouldn't mind saying I'd been wrong – if I had been. But it wouldn't make any difference – now. He doesn't want to marry me – and I can't marry a man who – who tries to force me to do something I feel is wrong – even if it turns out I was mistaken. I could be wrong all over the place, and it still wouldn't change that.'

'But he ain't that way, I tell you! He was mad, an' upset!'

'And I'm telling you he doesn't want to marry me now. He – he said it was – lucky – we found out about each other *in time*! And he went back on his promise.'

'He ain't no worse than you – you went back on your promise to him.'

'I? What promise?'

'You promised to marry him, an' you got all het up an' changed your mind. That's just what he done. Seems to me it's six of one and half a dozen of the other.'

'Oh, golly,' said Sue wearily. 'It's no use, Marianna. What's done is done.'

'Okay. You're the boss. Could you go to sleep now?'

'I – I'll try. And thanks a lot, Marianna. You've been sweet.'

'Aw, that's all right. I just happened to be passin'. G'night.'

'Good night.'

18
Festus

In a familiar house, where everything is as it has always been, it is hard to realize that your world has changed – especially when you are just emerging from sleep.

Sue woke in the morning to the sound of Marianna's sweeping. Water was running in the bathroom. The morning sunlight lay in its customary square at the corner of the room. Sue stared at it comfortably, feeling nothin, remembering nothing. Then she stretched; her hand encountered the damp ball of her handkerchief, and misery fell upon her in a dark avalanche.

She wasn't going to marry Bill!

But she had always been going to marry Bill. Her whole life was planned around it – centred on it. Now she had no plan and no centre. Everything that was vital was gone.

She got up quickly, finding relief in the simple everyday process of dressing.

This wasn't like last time – when she thought she had lost Bill, when she believed that he was falling in love with someone else. Beneath that wretchedness there had been a little hope. She hadn't realized it then, but she realized it now – when there was no hope. For this time Bill really didn't want to marry her.

'It's – as if he'd – died!' she thought, fumbling with her collar. She'd have to change all her habits of thinking. For now, whichever way her mind turned, it came up against that wall, and she would have to accept it as one accepts a death – because there is nothing else to do. At breakfast it was evident that Kit knew, for she didn't remark on Sue's pallor, and asked no questions about last night. 'Marianna told her,' Sue thought dully. 'So I won't have to. She'll understand if I don't say anything.'

Kit's only comment was made in the underground while the girls were waiting for their trains.

'I'm *frightfully* sorry, Bat!' That was all – just the affectionate touch of the old nickname.

The nurses at the office, however, were facetious about Sue's listlessness and lack of colour. She must have been up all night for a week, they said – or had somebody knocked her out with an old shoe at the wedding?

Sue tried to grin.

Miss Farrar called her back as she was leaving.

'I've got a new job for you if you'd like it,' she said. 'Miss Glines is coming off Mothers' Club. Would you be interested in taking her place?'

'Why, yes, I'd like to very much.'

'That's splendid! The course covers ten weeks of lectures, and if you stay around and do the refreshments and observe, then you can take over the next series.'

Sue nodded. 'Miss Farrar,' she said abruptly, 'what happens if a nurse decides to leave when she's only been at Henry Street a short time – six months?'

'She just resigns – giving a month's notice.'

'You – you mean – when she's only just got her training – and nobody thinks it isn't fair?'

'Of *course* not! Whatever gave you such an idea? You aren't thinking of leaving, are you?'

'No,' said Sue. 'I expect to be here – all my life! But other medical organizations have a fit if you don't stay on at least two years when you take a job – and I – somebody said down at Henry Centre that a nurse isn't really any good until she's been carrying her bag for a year or more. So I guess I had the impression that it was considered a low trick to walk out the minute you get your training.'

'Heavens, no! Miss MacDonald is very emphatic about that. She wants the nurses to feel absolutely free. They can go at any time. It's part of the Henry Street policy.'

'Oh!' said poor Sue. It was scarcely more than a whisper.

Miss Farrar smiled absently and turned her attention to the pile of papers on her desk. 'The new Mothers' Club,' she said, 'begins next Thursday.'

And so, on Thursday, Sue started on a new line of Public Health work.

During the intervening week she had had time to pull herself together a little – and to digest the appalling fact that she had wrecked everything by her stupidity in not learning Henry Street's real attitude on the subject of resignations.

'I suppose it was because I didn't want to leave,' she told herself, desperately honest. 'I took for granted what I *wanted* to be true. But I wasn't insincere! I didn't do that to Bill on purpose! I'd have left regardless, if I'd realized – and if he hadn't tried to make me! I'm not a cheat. And if I was dumb – so was Kit. She thought the same way that I did – and *she* certainly had no axe to grind. Oh, Bill, dear –'

None of this, however, altered the fact that Bill had been dictatorial – had tried to make her do something she honestly believed to be unethical. 'He might just as well have held me up at the point of a gun,' she thought, and was outraged anew.

These flashes of anger were wholesome in their effect, for they kept up Sue's flagging spirits. One cannot be utterly crushed, and angry at the same time, and though there were periods when Sue felt that nothing in the world mattered, or would ever matter again, that bracing sense of outrage came to her rescue sooner or later.

She longed to tell her mother the whole miserable story – but letters seldom make things quite clear. When she went home for her holiday she would tell them both – Mother and Dad. 'For there's time and to spare,' she thought bitterly. Meanwhile, Kit and Marianna were being very understanding – and it helped.

Marianna, gruffing and huffing, had done a really lovely thing in her effort to please and cheer Sue. She came home late a night or two after Bill had left, and stood about with an uneasiness that wasn't at all like Marianna – whose poise was not often upset. She eyed Sue uncertainly, wandered out to the kitchen, returned, seemed about to speak, said nothing. After fifteen minutes of this, Sue, unable to stand it any longer, said, 'For goodness' *sake*, Marianna! Are you trying to hypnotize me, or are you just playing Quaker Meeting?'

Marianna flushed. 'Aw!' she said. 'I was – just thinkin'. I – I got sump'n to tell you, an' I don't know how to begin.'

'What?' Sue put down the book she had not been reading.

'Well – I been some place to-night – I done it for you – sorter. Of course, I didn't really. I done it for myself. But I thought maybe you'd be kinder glad. That's doin' it for myself, ain't it? I mean, I'd be glad if you was glad – sorter.'

'Yes?' Sue encouraged her.

'Er – well.' Marianna took a deep breath and plunged. 'I – I've signed up to go to night school in September. I – I'm gonna be a nurse – some day.'

'*Marianna!*' Sue shrieked. 'You darling! Kit! Did you hear? Marianna's going to night school!'

'An' get to be a nurse,' Marianna put in firmly.

'Yes – and get to be a nurse! Oh, Marianna, I'm so glad! You knew I'd be, didn't you?'

Marianna nodded and arranged her features in an expression of ferocity. ''Tain't nothin',' she said.

Kit clattered down the stairs, glanced at Sue, and said briskly, 'Come on – we'll celebrate! We'll go to Radio City – my treat! Cheers for Marianna!'

Sue was deeply touched by Marianna's decision, guessing what it cost to give in about going to school; for Marianna was as unyielding as iron. But it was an ill wind that blew nobody any good, and this would be the making of Marianna. Once she had set herself to a task she would finish it – though what kind of nurse she would make was uncertain.

So, between the girls and her work, Sue kept her chin up. The Mothers' Club was more than helpful in this respect, not only because it was new to Sue, and interesting, but because of one of the patients, who kept the nurses in gales of laughter – and laughter was very good for Sue just now.

The purpose of the club was to teach expectant mothers how to take care of themselves before the baby was born, and how to take care of the baby as soon as it arrived.

They had lectures on the growth of the unborn child from its beginning to its birth. They were taught what to eat, how to exercise, what to wear, and how to make clothes, both for themselves and for the baby, from patterns given them at the club. They learned to read thermometers. They were taught what things were necessary for the baby's toilet and how to use them, and why. There were cards, each with a coloured picture on it of some article of food healthy for mother and baby, and the mothers could plan menus from them, choosing by picture whatever they preferred. There was a doll, the exact size of a new-born baby, which served as a model for the bath, and the mothers practised bathing it until they were skilful.

On the first day of the club meeting, and every third week thereafter, each mother was called into the next room by the assisting nurses and asked if anything was troubling her, if she needed help of any kind, if she had any complaints or unusual symptoms.

At each meeting, after the lecture and discussion, refreshments were served – tea and sandwiches and little cakes, all of which, of course, were free, as was the series of lectures.

Miss Glines, whose place Sue would take later,

gave the lectures, with Sue and Mrs Egan in attendance. Mrs Egan had charge of the records, and Sue managed the refreshments. They combined on the conferences with the mothers.

Every Henry Street branch had its Mothers' Club, but Sue had not had any experience along this line at Henry Centre, though, like all the nurses, she often sent patients from her district to the club.

The members came, however, from many other sources. The Maternity Clinics in the neighbourhood always sent their patients to the Mothers' Club, having found that women who attended the club did better, both mentally and physically, when the baby was born. Doctors sent their patients. Social workers came with cases. The patients themselves brought friends who were having babies. Often women who had heard of the club came to it because they were lonely and wanted to make friends. But for whatever reason they came, they remained, fascinated, and worked hard for the diploma given to each at the end of the course.

The class met in one of the lecture rooms of the Medical Centre, sitting wherever they pleased in the semicircular tiers of seats going up toward the back.

Twenty prospective mothers straggled in on Thursday and signed the register – twenty women, some in shabby mended clothes, some expensively dressed. Some were college graduates; others could barely read. They were Irish, Jewish, black, and plain American, and they sat side by side, sewing or knitting, and commenting freely on everything. It was all jolly, friendly, and informal.

Sue enjoyed the work immensely, but it gave her

some bad moments. A Mothers' Club of this kind, in Springdale, would have been her strongest hold on the faith and trust of the people there – and it would have been *such* a help to Bill in his work! The living-room of their home would – Sue swallowed. There'd never be a home, now – ever! She mustn't forget again. She must think of something else – and quickly.

The personalities of the women in the club were, of course, as varied as their nationalities, and Sue was interested in Miss Glines's method of handling them.

One woman, on the first day, announced in a hissing, shamefaced whisper to Sue that she had 'come for certain information.' Sue referred her to Miss Glines. The matter turned out to be merely a question of whether or not the abdomen of the mother should be bound after the baby came, but the woman seemed very much embarrassed.

Miss Glines, promptly and pleasantly, in the most matter-of-fact way, took it up with the entire club. The woman, startled at first by this open discussion of the physical, quickly adopted the same attitude, and her shamefacedness vanished.

There was a stout, noisy woman who became the club pest, interrupting everybody, and disagreeing with every opinion. Miss Glines was amiable, firm, and patient, remarking in Sue's ear that there was sure to be one pest in every class, and there was no good worrying about it.

There was a seventeen-year-old girl, married four months and already deserted by her husband. She took no part in the activities of the club, and Sue wondered why she came, since she didn't seem to understand anything of what went on.

'The poor kid comes,' said Miss Glines, 'because she's lonely and frightened and hungry. It's fun here. Every one is nice to her, and she gets something to eat.'

There was a sixteen-year-old Jewish girl, pretty, and cheaply overdressed, who sat listening, big-eyed, her jaws moving rhythmically on her gum. Sue wondered what she was thinking. She had probably rushed into marriage with some boy under the impression that it would be a lark, an exciting game – something to make the other girls look up to her. And now she was faced with heavy responsibilities and grim facts. 'Poor baby,' Sue thought. 'I bet she feels as if she'd stepped on a stair that wasn't there.'

The prize patient, however, was a Mrs Nixerine Sprinkler. She was an immense woman, very black, very shiny, and very hearty. She announced, the first day, that she had come, not because she needed instruction, but because 'it gets awful monogamous stickin' aroun' home.' She talked gaily and incessantly.

'Is that a bonnet you're making?' the little Jewish girl asked her.

'You bet! Ah kin make bonnets faster'n anything else. Ah got ten made, a'ready.'

'But ain't it awful small for a bonnet? I thought babies' heads were bigger than that. That wouldn't hardly cover a orange.'

The bonnet was passed from hand to hand, and everyone agreed it was too small.

Mrs Sprinkler stuck to her guns. 'No suh! It ain't too small. A baby's head ain't no bigger than that. Ah knows! Ah've had foah!'

Miss Glines laughed. 'Maybe,' she said; 'but if you have a nine-pound boy that cap will never fit him.'

'*Him!* 'Tain't no him! This baby's goin' to be a girl, wid a mighty small haid!'

Mrs Sprinkler arrived late at the second lecture. She was out of breath and her heart was pounding.

Miss Glines took her blood pressure – which was terrific. 'You ought to be home in bed,' Miss Glines told her.

'No suh! Ain't nawthin' th' matter wid *me*! Ah was rushed, that's all. Ah hed to beat all foah mah boys befo' Ah left.' She stopped, breathless. Then she added, 'No need shake yore haids like that! There's mo' pishchology in the end ob a stick than you gets in all yore books! An' if Ah hadn' of beat Festus Ah wouldn' be so done up.'

'Which,' said the delighted nurses, 'is Festus?'

'He mah oldes' boy – twenty-one, an' a sight too big fo' lickin' – but Ah don' know what else to do.'

'Why? What's the matter with Festus?'

Festus, it seemed, wouldn't work. Mrs Sprinkler had found him jobs, but he refused them. He was big, handsome, and good natured – but he wouldn't work.

'Ah tole him, Ah says, "Festus Sprinkler, you kin sleep in this house, an' you kin eat what yore brothers eats. But I ain' goin' buy yore clo'es. You kin work for 'em!" He laks good clo'es, Festus does. But he don' work – an' he pick he clo'es outa trash cans. When Ah lams him one, he ack lak Ah's his best girl – comes snogglin' aroun' me, a-grinnin'.'

'Here's a problem for you, Barton,' Miss Glines said to Sue. 'They're in your district.'

Sue called on Mrs Sprinkler a day or two later, and

interviewed Festus. He was tall and black, with a delightful smile and very nice manners.

Sue spoke tentatively about work.

'Ma'am,' said Festus amiably, 'there ain't a bit of sense in work. Look at Paw. He's been workin' all his life an' all he's got is tired. He makes out he likes it, but he don't. Nobody likes to work – they just do it on account of they ain't got brains enough not to.'

Sue laughed. 'But they have to eat, you know.'

'Well, Ah'm eatin', ain't I?'

'You wouldn't even take a job for a week?'

'No, ma'am, certainly not.'

But Sue could be persistent, too. And whenever she heard of a possible job she offered it to Festus. He pointed out pleasantly that the cheese factory smelled. Would she like that kind of job herself?

'I'd take it if I couldn't get anything better.'

'But Ah've got somethin' better. Ah got nothin' to do!'

'Festus – you're hopeless.'

He continued to be hopeless. It was too hot to dig ditches, too damp to work in the underground. Sue gave up.

In October Mrs Sprinkler reported to the Mothers' Club that Festus was going from bad to worse. 'He's runnin' wid a low-life crowd,' she said. 'Ah cain't do nawthin' wid him. Ah cain't even catch him to beat him.' She moaned – a good lusty moan. 'Effen he'd git to work he wouldn't have no mind for caperin'.'

The entire club was in hearty agreement with this, but they were all aware that you cannot force a twenty-one-year-old boy to work if he doesn't want to. He was of age, and legally free to do as he chose.

But they were all interested and full of suggestions. Mrs Sprinkler had the floor at every meeting.

Towards the last of October Mrs Sprinkler's baby was born – at home – and she had to leave the club before the lectures were quite finished.

'Now Ah won't git me no diploma,' she wailed. 'Ah was all set for it. Ah ain't never graduated from nothin' till now – an' now Ah ain't.'

'Don't worry,' Miss Glines told her. 'You'll get your diploma.'

So Mrs Sprinkler retired, happy.

Sue went to see her after the baby came, to help with the first bath. The baby was a girl, weighing five pounds, and had a small head.

'She ain't big enough to make a good roastin' chicken,' Mrs Sprinkler said proudly.

Festus was still lounging around the house, cheerful and contented, and Sue longed to shake him, though she said nothing.

That afternoon, however, making a visit in the same street, Sue beheld a long yellow sports roadster rolling smoothly up to the Sprinklers' door. It glittered with chromium. Its horn played a tune. At the wheel sat Festus.

He handled the car beautifully, with the skill of a born driver, weavin in and out among lorries and children with effortless ease. Beside him, admiring, sat a slim brown girl in a mink coat.

The car came to a stop. Festus relinquished the wheel and stepped out of the car, ragged and casual and completely master of the situation.

Heads appeared in windows. Children gathered. Pretty girls paused to stare – at the mink coat, and at Festus. Their eyes rested longest on Festus.

He went up the dingy steps with his usual non-chalance, and the eyes of the brown girl in the car followed him. 'So long, honey,' she called after him wistfully.

Festus turned with his charming smile.

'So long,' he said, and continued on up the steps.

Sue hurried across the street after him.

'Wait, Festus!'

Festus removed his torn cap and grinned at her, white teeth gleaming in his dark face.

'How do, Miss Barton! Got me another of them jobs, Ah'll bet.'

'No, I haven't, Festus, but I saw you going by in that lovely car. I didn't know you could drive, and I wanted to tell you I think you do it beauti-fully.'

'Thank you, ma'am. Ah'm a better driver than any chauffeur.' He was not boasting. It was a simple statement of fact.

Sue was doing some quick thinking. Miss Farrar knew a Board of Health doctor who had just bought a new car, and was looking for a chauffeur.

'But, Festus,' she said, 'why didn't you tell me you could drive?' She laughed suddenly, and a twinkle came into the boy's eyes.

'It's a comin',' he said. 'But Ah ain't takin' any. I don't want to work in no garages, an' I ain't goin' to drive a lorry.'

'But would you like to drive a beautiful, expensive car – as chauffeur?'

'Why yes,' said Festus languidly. 'Ah might. Ah'd give it my consideration, anyways.'

'Honestly, you're the most maddening – Why

didn't you tell me, when I was trying to get you work, that you'd take a chauffeur's job?'

Festus grinned at her as if she were a small child. 'Ah was gettin' around to it,' he said soothingly.

19
Miss Weston's Dream

November was an unpleasant month, windy and rainy, with heavy skies, and Harlem was inexpressibly dreary. Sue tried not to think about Springdale, high in the fresh clear air of the mountain. There would be snow there soon, reaching white fingers down the mountain sides and drifting across the valleys. The people would have to struggle with it, but they would not have to struggle with overcrowding and dirt.

It was strange and a little frightening to find herself still looking for a letter on the hall table, when she came in at night. She ought to be getting over that – and she ought to stop writing letters to Bill in her mind. She was always doing it – always thinking of little things that would amuse him. The sentences formed themselves and she saw them on the page in spite of all her efforts to the contrary. It had never occurred to her that she might cease to love Bill. She knew that she would always love him, and she accepted the fact. The problem was to become accustomed to living without him, and this grew more, instead of less, difficult as time went on. Small things were what made the trouble: the letter that never came; her bankbook, reminding her of the cheque Dad had sent to buy her trousseau; the little chain on which she had worn Bill's ring, lying tangled in her glove box; a old envelope with a Springdale postmark on it. Everywhere she turned there was something to add to the weight of realization. She grew tired with it and more listless, except when she was working.

At Thanksgiving she caught a cold and missed both the Mothers' Club celebration and the giving away of the Thanksgiving baskets at the Settlement.

'What you need,' said Kit briskly, 'is a good rest, or anyway a change. You're dragging around like a rheumatic joint. Why don't you ask for a couple of weeks off in a lump, instead of staying home a day at a time?'

'Oh, because –' said Sue vaguely. She didn't want to stop work and lie around and think.

'You could go up and stay with George and Eleanor,' Kit urged. 'They'd adore it, and we've scarcely seen them this autumn. Or you might go up and see Connie and Phil. They must be over the first throes by this time.' She didn't suggest that Sue went home – to New Hampshire.

'I'm all right.'

'Oh, my, yes! The way you throw off a cold is miraculous! Give you another year and we'll hardly know you have a cold! It'll be just a noisy dew, as the Californian said of the thunderstorm.'

Sue grinned behind her handkerchief. 'If I'm so feeble, how about letting me have that couch?'

'Because you ought to be in bed,' said Kit, not moving.

Marianna came in with wood for the fireplace and sent a shower of sparks up the little chimney. Then she vanished upstairs to study.

'What do you bet,' said Kit, 'that she does the

four-year course in two?' She got up suddenly. 'Oh, take your darned couch. I didn't want it anyway.'

'Thanks. Have a chair. I can recommend it. And I'm not betting. Marianna's got a mind like a steel trap and I've no doubt she'll do the four years in two. She's had two months of English and she's shedding bad grammar as if it were dead fleas.'

'That's a charming, delicate simile. Marianna would be gratified.'

They fell silent, staring at the fire.

Sue's cold lingered on into December in the form of a cough, which she ignored. She was busy – with the Mothers' Club, with influenza in her district, with preparations for Christmas.

The Washington Heights office, having no settlement house, and being merely an office, did not give a Christmas party as did most of the other Centres. But there would be a great fragrant pile of Christmas trees to be given away. And there would be presents, wrapped by the Girl Guides and distributed by the nurses to sick children in their districts.

For days Sue had been checking over and adding to her list of families needing food, clothing, and toys, to be referred to the social agencies. She had also been thinking a great deal about Miss Weston.

Miss Weston didn't need food or clothing. Her teacher's pension provided her with necessities. She didn't need toys, for she was seventy and unmarried and her sister's children were grown up. She didn't even need a Christmas tree given her. She could buy it herself.

Miss Weston had influenza and her doctor had sent for a Henry Street nurse. Sue went.

Miss Weston lived in a large, pleasantly furnished room lined with books on travel and history. The wall was covered with maps, and the bed was strewn with brightly coloured travel folders which rose to a mountainous peak in Miss Weston's lap.

She was a large, angular woman with snow-white hair, faded blue eyes, and a lovely vibrant voice, extraordinarily young in timbre for a woman of seventy.

Sue inquired about the steamship folders.

Miss Weston's faded old eyes brightened. 'Oh, those,' she said in her young voice. 'They're the dream that will never come true.' There was no bitterness in her voice – only resignation. She picked absently at the bedspread for a moment. 'You see,' she went on, 'I'm one of those people who seem to have been born with a wanderlust – and I've never been outside the state of New York. When I was young I was sure that each year I could go – but there was always something.'

'You mean you never had a chance to go anywhere?'

'Well, yes.' She was almost apologetic. 'I tried; I saved and planned. But first my sister had to be educated. That was when I gave up the idea of India and China. Then my mother had a long illness and several operations. That took the money I'd saved for Europe. After my sister married and Father and Mother – passed on, I saved enough to go to Central America.' She paused.

'Yes?' said Sue gently.

'My – my sister's husband borrowed it for an investment. He – lost it. I was getting on in years, but I thought I might be able to see Mexico at least.' She sighed. 'I guess it wasn't to be. I had a good many illnesses myself. So now that I'm an old woman I go travelling on steamship folders.'

'But what do you *do* with them?'

'Oh, I plan trips. I decide where I'll go, first. Then I read about the places in books of travel. Sometimes' – she flushed. – 'I – I'm afraid I even read cheap adventure stories.'

Sue hadn't the least desire to smile. 'But the folders?' she said.

'Oh, they come last – when it's time to arrange my itinerary, and choose my stateroom. At first I used to go on the cheaper of the conducted tours. I couldn't spend much, you know, and I always tried to keep within my means. But conducted tours can be very tiresome, and then, too, the more you travel, the more experienced you become. Now I go off by myself – on freighters and tramp steamers.'

The trips were utterly real to her – so real that for the moment they became so to Sue, who asked, without any feeling that her question was fantastic, 'Aren't you afraid to do that? I should think it would be dangerous.'

'Oh no! The freighters are perfectly safe, and very comfortable. Of course, they're slow – they stop for weeks sometimes, in a port – but that gives me a chance to go ashore, and live on the boat at the same time. It's very cheap that way.'

Sue's first idea, after this talk, was that Miss Weston had a lot of fun, travelling around in her imagination. But she changed her mind a day or two later.

The weather was raw and cold and Sue came in chilled through in spite of her heavy coat.

'My dear!' Miss Weston exclaimed. 'Make yourself a cup of coffee at once – you're blue with cold! You'll find the jug on the pantry shelf.'

Sue retired to the pantry. 'There are two jugs of coffee here,' she called. 'They both look alike. Which–?'

'Just bring one here.'

Sue brought the jug to the bed. Miss Weston took it from her, opened it, and drew a deep lungful of the spicy air inside.

'This is the one,' she said. Then, suddenly, 'Did you ever really think about the smell of coffee, Miss Barton?' She didn't wait for an answer. 'Coffee,' she repeated. 'Coffee – growing in hot lands under the equator – carried through steaming jungles – heaped in fragrant pyramids in the holds of ships that smell of tar and the sea. Wind sings in the ropes and roars in the funnels –' The beautiful voice broke. 'I'm a fool!' Miss Weston said. 'A childish old fool!'

'Oh, no!' Sue cried. 'Please don't say that!'

'But I am, my dear. I torture myself with longing for something I shall never have. I'm an old woman. My life is nearly done, and I shall go to my grave without ever having set foot outside New York State. I shall never see the jungle, or hear the wind singing across three thousand miles of blue ocean! I shall never see anything – anything at all – and I am a fool not to face it.'

'I'm terribly sorry, Miss Weston.'

'Never mind, child.' She lay back against her pillows, her face suddenly drawn and tired. 'I'm just a fretful old woman. Forget what I have said.'

But Sue didn't forget it. And one day she spoke to Miss Farrar about it. 'It's so – so unfair,' she concluded. 'There are organizations to feed people, and clothe them, and nurse them, and get them jobs. There are scholarships for the young, and pensions for the old – but there isn't *any* help for this kind of thing! She'll die without ever having lived – because that's what living is, to her.'

'I'm not so sure,' said Miss Farrar, 'that something couldn't be done. There *is* an agency which has a fund for people like that – unusual people. Go and see them. Here – I'll give you the address.'

Sue went in wild excitement, Miss Weston's white hair before her against a background of purple mountains and green jungle. 'If I never do anything else,' Sue cried in her thoughts, 'I'll be satisfied to have done this!'

Central America would be best. It was nearest. The name alone brought up pictures of Maya cities, buried and forgotten, of crimson parrots, of palm trees against the sky – all the things Miss Weston yearned to see. And it wouldn't be so very expensive. Surely, they'd give her the trip – when they knew. They must!!

On the way, Sue paused to telephone a steamship company whose vessels went to the Caribbean.

A pleasant masculine voice answered. Yes, there were ships sailing every other week to Jamaica, Puerto Barrios, Puerto Cortés, Guatemala, and Honduras. The round trip took twelve days. The price was from one hundred and fifty dollars up.

It was too good to be true, Sue thought.

And she was right; for the agency was very sympathetic but very sorry. If the trip were for the purpose of establishing the lady in business, or reuniting her with her family, it would be different. But they couldn't send somebody to Central America just for the fun of it. It must be a necessity of some kind.

'But it *is* a necessity!' Sue cried.

'I'm sorry, but I'm afraid it isn't the right kind of a necessity. Of course, if you could find someone to put up the money, we will be glad to administer it. Otherwise –'

Sue left the office miserably depressed. It would have been better, she thought, if she had never begun to plan for now she couldn't bear to give up. Well, apparently this was her year for giving up – everything.

Ten days before Christmas Sue wrote to her mother about Bill. She couldn't stand any more affectionate maternal references to the future – when that particular future would never be. Her mother's reply came on Sue's afternoon off. She took it upstairs and curled up on the bed before she opened it. It was distressed but sympathetic.

. . . I suppose you know best, dear. But we are all so sorry. We like him so much. Your father wishes me to say that if it will cheer you up he hopes you will do something foolish. I'm sure I can't think what he means, but he said you'd understand. Only do be careful, dear. Your father has such wild notions at times and you're very like him.

Ted says . . .

Sue laughed tenderly at this characteristic epistle. She knew exactly what Dad meant. And he knew exactly what she needed. But she couldn't think of anything foolish to do.

'I can't spend my substance in riotous living because I haven't any substance – except the money Dad gave me for my trousseau, and that – *great jumping beans!*'

Sue rushed headlong down the stairs to the telephone. Miss Weston should have her trip! Dad's cheque had been for two hundred dollars – the people at the agency had said that if someone would put up the money – Miss Weston need never know who had done it – nobody would ever know who had done it!

The arrangements were made without difficulty, and a day or two later Sue climbed the stairs to Miss Weston's room with her heart pounding in her throat.

Miss Weston had been up and about for some time, and when Sue came in was sitting in the rocking chair by the window.

'Why, my dear child!' she said. 'How nice to see you. I hoped you wouldn't forget me, now I'm no longer your patient– Why, what is it, child? You look about to burst.'

'I'm not about to,' said Sue. 'I *am* bursting! See! I brought you a Christmas present.'

She took an envelope out of her pocket and handed it to Miss Weston, who opened it, round-eyed and pleased.

'What's all this?' she said. 'Guatemala – oh! Are you having a holiday?'

'I'm not – but you are!'

'*I*? What do you mean?'

'I mean that I went to an agency which has a fund for people like you. The agency arranged everything. And so, my dear Miss Weston, on the day before Christmas, no less, you are sailing on the *Santa Rita* for a twelve-day cruise to Central America and the Caribbean.'

Miss Weston's face was white and still. She looked from Sue to the green ticket with her name upon it. Then she said, very slowly, 'It's – going – to happen, then?' She paused, went on again in that strange, slow voice. 'On the day before Christmas – I – Alice Weston – am going to – to *sail*? I am – going to walk – up the gangway – of a boat – carrying a bag?'

'That's right.'

'You – you're sure? There – couldn't – be a mistake?'

'There isn't any mistake, Miss Weston, dear. You're really and truly going – and I'm going to see you off.'

'I'm really and truly going,' Miss Weston repeated. 'I'm sailing. Alice Weston is sailing. That's me.'

Sue watched the dawning of realization in the old eyes. And then suddenly, to Sue's distress, Miss Weston carefully, and with dignity, folded her arms on the window sill, laid her head upon them, and burst into tears.

Sue waited patiently and after a time perceived that Miss Weston was saying something in a muffled voice. Sue bent over her. 'What?'

'I – I said – there will be monkeys.'

'Goodness! Why, yes.'

Miss Weston sat up. Her lips still trembled and her eyes were wet, but they were no longer the eyes of an old woman – they were as young as her voice, deeply blue, and shining. She wiped them with the back of her hand, and cleared her throat.

'I shall bring one back,' she said firmly.

'One what?'

'Monkey. Even if I have to – to steal it!'

Sue laughed shakily. 'You won't have to. Look! There's a cheque!'

'Cheque! Oh, Miss Barton – what for?'

'For you to spend as foolishly as possible.'

'Get my glasses, child, quickly – there on the table! That's it. Thank you, dear.' She picked up the cheque and gasped. '*Fifty dollars!* Oh, Miss Barton! I – I've never spent any money foolishly.' She paused, then added, 'But I bet I can learn.'

'I'll bet you can – and I hope you do!'

They laughed like children together, and then Sue went away on her round of visits, happier than she had been in a long while.

'That's the best job I ever did,' she thought. 'And was it ever worth it! All I ask is to see her going up the gangway with her bag – and if she doesn't come home with a monkey I'll never speak to her again!'

It would have been fun to tell the girls, but no one must know about the money – except Dad, who would adore the whole thing. Now, if only the day before Christmas could manage to be clear and pleasant.

The day before Christmas, however, turned out to be anything but pleasant. A wet snow began to fall sometime during the night, and it fell all day, melting into a thick slush. Miss Weston's boat sailed at noon, and Sue, loaded with books and sweets, went down to see it off, getting there just in time to pass them over the side – and too late to go on board.

Miss Weston's white hair towered above the crowd at the deck rail, her eyes deep wells of excitement, but her manner calm, as was fitting in so experienced a traveller.

The gangway swung up and in and a band began to play. There was a rattle of chains – shouts – a long, roaring, and triumphant whistle.

Sue watched the glowing face under the crown of white hair – a young face now, vibrant with life and happiness. The ship trembled, and then, imperceptibly, the black line of water began to widen between it and the dock. Miss Weston stared at the withdrawing pier, her whole face quivering with emotion too deep for words or gesture.

Sue turned and ran along the dock to its end, to stand ankle-deep in slush, and wave. Miss Weston should have all the trimmings!

When the ship was a dark hulk fading into the driving snow, and Miss Weston's flourishing handkerchief could not be distinguished from a hundred other handkerchiefs, Sue awoke to the fact that she was wet through, and that her teeth were chattering with the beginning of a furious chill.

'This is simply ducky!' she though, turning up her collar and jamming her freezing hands into her pockets. 'I throw a fit of nobility and unselfishness and what does it get me? The spotted death at the very least!'

She gave one last look at the ship, on its way to the warm southlands with Miss Weston. Then she turned and trudged back through the grey slush of the pier to the greyer slush of the city streets.

20
Marianna Interferes

Sue tried to work that afternoon with the growing tightness in her chest, but at three o'clock she gave up, telephoned Miss Farrar, and went home to bed. Kit and Marianna found her there, sodden, when they came home.

'This is dandy,' said Kit. 'Where did you get it?'

'Hanging around a Hudson River pier,' Sue croaked. 'It's a reward for virtue.'

'You must have been unbearably virtuous. What on earth were you doing over there? Trying to get sunstroke?'

'Not at all! I just went to see how it was.'

'How was it?'

'The mosquitoes were pretty bad, but otherwise it was fine.'

'It must have been. Did you have a hot bath?'

'On the pier? Certainly not!'

'Well, you're going to have one now! Start the tub, Marianna, will you. Make it blistering! I'm going to heat blankets.'

They scalded Sue in the tub, and smothered her in hot blankets. They filled her with lemonade, and honey and hot water, and pineapple juice, and plain and fancy tea.

The camomile tea was the last straw.

'Go right away, Marianna,' said Sue hoarsely. 'I

won't take it!'

'Aw, come on!'

'No! Enough is enough! I splash every time I move. I feel like a water mattress! And if you think I'm going to drink a lot of dead flowers out of a hayfield – you're wrong!'

'You'd better drink it,' said Kit, hovering, 'and lie down and keep quiet. You're getting hoarser and hoarser. Honestly, Sue – *please*. You won't have a speck of voice to-morrow.'

'I'm not hoarse! I'm just gargling through the flood. If my voice is gone to-morrow it'll be because my vocal cords have turned into seaweed!'

'For heaven's sake, *will* you hush? You'll be simply dead in the morning!'

'Yes, drowned. Just wire my sorrowing relatives to send pond lilies for the remains.'

They got her quiet at last.

'I'll leave the hall light on,' Kit told her, 'and if you want a drink or anything –'

'A drink!'

'– just call me. Don't go bouncing out of bed in a dripping perspiration. Good night, old thing.'

'G'night,' Sue murmured drowsily. Then she stirred and sat up. 'What *are* you doing, Marianna? I mean – must you?'

Marianna was fidgeting and made no reply. She moved the wastebasket. She shut the cupboard door. She picked up a scrap of paper. She brought Sue another handkerchief, and at last she moved across to the window to open it, and remained staring out at the falling snow.

Sue watched her for a moment and then lay down.

You could do nothing with Marianna when she was in one of these moods – except leave her alone.

'To-morrow is Christmas,' Marianna said at last.

'I suppose so.'

Marianna turned and looked at her. 'Do you wish it wasn't?'

'Why, no. I don't see what difference it makes. Why?'

'Oh, nothing. I was just thinking.'

There was an odd quality, a kind of urgency, in Marianna's voice.

'What were you thinking, Marianna?'

'Oh, a whole bunch of things. It don't – doesn't matter.'

'Tell me.'

'Well, I was thinking you felt that way – that it didn't make n – any difference about it being Christmas. And I was thinking you aren't such a bad egg – when you come right down to it. And I was thinking about me being here.'

'I'm glad you're here.'

'Well, you never can tell,' said Marianna strangely, and went out.

Sue woke later, feeling stifled, and sat up fighting the bedclothes, still half asleep. Kit appeared, wraith-like, at the bedside.

'You all right, Bat?'

'No – yes – I don't know. I'm pretty stuffy.'

'You'd better have an inhalation. It'll clear you out.' Kit was gone before Sue could protest, but she was downstairs only a few minutes, and she returned empty-handed. 'Sue – Marianna isn't here!'

'Isn't here!' said Sue blankly.

'No. And her bed hasn't been touched. What do you think?'

'Golly, Kit! I don't know! But I'm sure it's all right. What time is it?'

'Not very late – only about midnight. But why would she go out like that, without saying anything?'

'I haven't the least idea. But after all, it's Christmas Eve. Maybe she's going to spring a Christmas surprise on us. She's an awful kid, at heart.'

'Maybe that's it. And she can't have been out long, because it was nearly eleven when I came upstairs, and she was hanging icicles on the tree, then.'

'Oh, she's all right – don't worry.'

Sue felt better after the inhalation, but she was no longer sleepy, and she was awake when Marianna's key grated in the front-door lock. Sue smiled in the darkness. 'I'll bet it's some kid trick,' she thought. She would have called out a 'Merry Christmas,' but her voice was too croaky to be intelligible.

It was worse than croaky in the morning. It had gone entirely, and the cold was in her nose, as well.

'Oh, I feel fide,' she told the girls in a loud whisper. 'Berry Chrizbus! Habby Dew Year! See whad your fluids did for me! Add thad dice hod bath.'

'Oh, Sue!' Kit wailed. 'It's Christmas morning, and look at you!'

'You loog! I'b dod ideresded! Has id sdopped sdowing?'

'What?'

'Sue says,' Marianna put in, 'has it stopped snowing? Sure it has. It's a swell day out.'

'Do you feel very awful, Sue?'

'Sodder.'

'Golly! We were supposed to go up to George and Eleanor's – but you can't go anywhere.'

'You go,' Sue whispered.

'Go on, Kit,' Marianna urged. 'I'll stay with her. I – I don't feel so good myself.'

She was really pale, and Kit glanced at her sharply. Nothing, however, was said about last night's odd disappearance, for the girls had never assumed any authority over Marianna, and since she didn't volunteer for an explanation they asked for none.

'What about opening our presents?' Kit said.

Marianna spoke quickly. 'Why don't we do it when you come back this afternoon? Sue'll prob'ly be kinder more alive by then.'

'Why, all right. But what's come over you, Marianna? You've been feeling those packages, and shaking 'em, for two days, and now, all of a sudden, you've lost the urge.'

'No, I ai – haven't. I just thought it would be nicer later. You go on up to the Craigs', Kit.'

'Here's your hat, what's your hurry?' Kit said suspiciously. 'Are you trying to get rid of me?'

'Oh, no!' said Marianna hastily.

They clattered downstairs, clattered up again with Sue's breakfast. Kit made her bed. Marianna brought her a book. But at last the front door closed behind Kit, and the house was quiet. Marianna remained downstairs.

Sue lay staring through the window at the hard blue of the sky until, made drowsy by a degree of temperature, she fell asleep.

She didn't know what woke her, but whatever it was she wished it hadn't, and she hoped Marianna would stay downstairs, and not come bothering around with drinks.

'No luck!' she thought a moment later, hearing Marianna's step on the stairs. The steps came across the little landing to the door and stopped.

She turned her head and every muscle in her body contracted with shock.

Bill was standing in the doorway.

His face was dead white and there were heavy circles under his eyes.

Sue opened her mouth but only a squeak emerged from it.

Bill came across the threshold and bent over the bed, an agony of tenderness in his face.

'Sue!' he said. 'It's Bill!'

Sue's mind was in a turmoil, devoid of thought or coherence. She could only look at him.

Bill spoke again, quickly – desperately – as if no words could be wasted.

'I came to say that I love you, and that I've been wrong. Will you forgive me?'

Sue was beyond wonder.

'*Will I ever!*' she whispered, and laid her hands in his.

Marianna's voice spoke suddenly from the hall. 'Bill,' it said, 'I got to tell you – she's only got a cold!'

'*What!*' It was a shout of wild relief. 'Marianna, you blessed little devil! Sue darling – *my God!*'

Marianna called out from the stairs. 'You'd've known in a minute anyway, soon's you had a good look at her – but I wanted to tell you myself.'

But Bill wasn't listening. 'Sue, dear,' he said. 'I – His voice broke.

'Whad is id, darlig? Whad did she do?'

He drew a crumpled telegram from his pocket and handed it to Sue.

It read:

SUE ILL STOP COME AT ONCE IF YOU WANT TO SEE HER
WHILE SHE IS STILL ABLE TO SPEAK
      MARIANNA

'It's – been horrible,' Bill said, 'but – it's worth it now! I did – just what she knew I'd do – believed you dying. And all the way in the plane –'

'*You flew?*'

'Of course I flew! What would you expect me to do? I got a plane at five this morning. And all the way I thought what it would mean if you. I – I nearly went crazy. I felt – that I loved you – that I was sorry. I'd wanted to tell you that long ago – but I thought you'd stopped loving me.' He paused, and then said slowly, 'That ceased to be a reason when I thought you were going to die. I had to tell you, that was all. And I want you to know, now, that any length of wait is better than never having you.

'I do'd thig you'll have to wait. Because I was rog.'

'You were what, darling?'

'Rog! You dow – *rog*!'

'Yes, surely. That's fine – but what is rog? It sounds like something out of *Sinbad the Sailor*.'

'Oh!' Sue wailed. 'Whad kide of a doctor are you, addyway? Ged be subthing for my doze quickly.'

'Of course!' He was at the door in one stride. 'I'll be right back!' The front door slammed.

'Marianna!' Sue called. 'You cobe here!'

Marianna came, a little frightened. 'Are you sore at me, Sue?'

'I adore you! Bud what gave you the idea?'

'Oh, that! Why, it was you and Kit talking all that stuff – remember – about you not being going to have any voice – and Kit saying you'd be dead – and then you said to wire your folks to send pond lilies.'

'Why did'd you just say cobe at wudse?'

'Because it was more awful about you not speaking, and I wanted to make sure he knew, really, how he felt.'

'You're a dadgerous wobad,' Sue whispered happily. 'Gee! I feel swell! Berry Chrisbus, everybody!'

'Then it's all right?'

'All righd? Id's wudderful!'

Bill returned with sprays and medicine, bounding up the stairs four at a time, and presently Sue was able to whisper with reasonable distinctness.

'Now then,' Bill said, 'what about this rog business?'

'Wrong, you lunatic! I was just trying to tell you I'd been wrong, too, about –'

'You weren't as wrong as I was. Nobody has any right to ride over other people's rules about living. I'm frightfully sorry, Sue. I'm not like that, really.'

'I know you aren't. Let's not think about all that any more – ever. No, you can't kiss me! I'm catching! And you haven't let me tell you what I was wrong about. I said you wouldn't have to wait. Because I was wrong about it being unethical to leave Henry Street – and you were right. Only, Bill, please believe me when I say I was perfectly sincere. I – I wouldn't do a thing like that to you, on purpose.'

'I know you wouldn't,' Bill said gently. 'But am I hearing right? Did you say I wouldn't have to wait – very long?'

She nodded.

They looked at one another mutely, and in that silence all the bitterness and pain of the last months vanished for ever.

'When?' Bill said at last.

'Can you stay over another day?'

'I can't, but I will.'

'Then I want you to come with me to see Miss MacDonald. We'll tell her the circumstances and she what she says. Maybe I can leave sooner than I think – and I think a month, anyway.'

'A month! *Sue*!'

'And there's one other thing I want.'

'It's yours! What is it?'

'Well,' Sue hesitated. 'Would you hate a wedding?'

'For gosh sake! What do you think I've been trying to bring you to, all this while?'

'But I mean a *real* wedding, in white tulle and smilax and everybody crying.'

Bill groaned. 'I know. You mean a *wedding*. With cheese scoops and funny lamps and twenty-five pickle forks and "Who's that feeble-minded-looking man over there? Oh! The groom!"'

Sue beamed. 'That's it exactly. I want everybody bellowing and saying "Isn't she lovely?" and the best man losing the ring and the bridesmaid being sick from excitement.'

'I'll even,' said Bill, 'supply the bridesmaid. My niece, Emily, is five years old, and she'd be glad to trip you coming up the aisle.'

'No aisle. I'm going to be married at home.'

'Oh, pardon me! My mistake! And speaking of home – I had been meaning to tell you – last summer, when – well, anyway, I – I had taken an option on a house for us. I still have it. I didn't want to buy until you'd seen it.'

'A *house*! Oh, *Bill*! What's it like?'

'Wait till you see it,' said the light-hearted Bill. And then, suddenly struck with an idea, 'Look here, what about Kit? This is going to be a rather lonely business for her.'

'Yes, it is! I feel pretty low about that, but I don't know what I can do.'

'Does she want to stay on at Henry Street?'

'Well, not indefinitely. She wants to be a hospital executive.'

Bill pondered. 'The nearest hospital to Springdale is fifty miles away. But it's a good little hospital with a very excellent training school. I'm sure I could get Kit a job there.'

'Did you say *training school*?'

'Yes. Why?'

'Because Marianna wants to be a nurse.' Sue's eyes shone. 'Oh, Bill – if Kit went there Marianna could be with her – and they'd both be near enough for weekends and afternoons off. It would be simply marvellous! She laughed suddenly. 'You know, I've wondered and wondered *what* kind of a nurse Marianna would make! Now I'll know.'

'You will if they want to go there.'

'They'll go all right. It's just the kind of thing Kit would love. And it would never occur to Marianna not to go with her if she were asked.'

Hand in hand, they smiled at one another, arranging their world to their satisfaction. There remained only the question of when Sue would leave – and Miss MacDonald would settle that.

Miss MacDonald settled it promptly, next day. She listened, smiling, to Bill's account of his work, and to Sue's eager explanations, saying nothing until they had finished.

'My dear child' – she turned to Sue – 'I think that's splendid! Of course, we'll be sorry to lose you – but that's the kind of thing we hope our nurses will do. That's what you've been trained for! Why you'll be a *pioneer* up in those mountains – and we'll be proud to say that you were a Henry Street nurse.'

'Th – thank you,' Sue stammered.

Miss MacDonald looked at Bill and her eyes twinkled. 'I suppose you want to know when, Dr Barry. We usually expect a month's notice from our nurses – but Miss Barton needs a rest, and I think two weeks' notice in this case will be enough.' She rose and held out her hand. 'I hope you'll both be very happy – together – and in your work!'

Her level glance followed them through the door, and she smiled again at the sound of their footsteps mingling in the old corridors. They were so young and so eager – starting out on their new life together.

Downstairs on the first floor Sue paused, and looked up with a faint gasp.

'Bill! My trousseau! I won't have any!'

'Who,' said Bill, 'cares about a trousseau! Come on! I'm going to send a wire to your father.'